Harvard
Business
Review

ON

LEADERSHIP IN A CHANGED WORLD

THE HARVARD BUSINESS REVIEW PAPERBACK SERIES

The series is designed to bring today's managers and professionals the fundamental information they need to stay competitive in a fast-moving world. From the preeminent thinkers whose work has defined an entire field to the rising stars who will redefine the way we think about business, here are the leading minds and landmark ideas that have established the *Harvard Business Review* as required reading for ambitious businesspeople in organizations around the globe.

Other books in the series:

Other books in the series (continued):

Harvard Business Review

ON

LEADERSHIP IN A CHANGED WORLD

A HARVARD BUSINESS REVIEW PAPERBACK

The *Harvard Business Review* articles in this collection are available as individual reprints. Discounts apply to quantity purchases. For information and ordering, please contact Customer Service, Harvard Business School Publishing, Boston, MA 02163. Telephone: (617) 783-7500 or (800) 988-0886, 8 A.M. to 6 P.M. Eastern Time, Monday through Friday. Fax: (617) 783-7555, 24 hours a day. E-mail: custserv@hbsp.harvard.edu

Library of Congress Cataloging-in-Publication Data
Harvard business review leadership in a changed world.
      p.   cm. — (The Harvard business review paperback)
    Includes index.
    ISBN 1-59139-501-1
    1. Social responsibility of business.   2. Globalization—Economic aspects.   3. Leadership.   4. International business enterprises—Management.   I. Harvard business review.   II. Series.
    HD60.H3893 2004
    658.4′092—dc22   2003023490
                                                                           CIP

The paper used in this publication meets the requirements of the American National Standard for Permanence of Paper for Publications and Documents in Libraries and Archives Z39.48–1992.

Contents

Harvard
Business
Review

ON

LEADERSHIP IN A CHANGED WORLD

Microcapitalism and the Megacorporation

DEBRA DUNN AND KEITH YAMASHITA

Executive Summary

MORE THAN 100 MILES FROM Bangalore, India, there's a rural area called Kuppam where one in three citizens is illiterate, more than half of the households have no electricity, and there's a high rate of AIDS. It's exactly this challenging atmosphere that prompted Hewlett-Packard to choose Kuppam as one of its first "i-communities" initiatives. Through the program, HP creates public – private partnerships to accelerate economic development through the application of technology while simultaneously opening new markets and developing new products and services.

HP brings to these initiatives the management disciplines of a successful technology business. For example, it unearths customer needs using an iterative cycle that involves prototyping products and services and then closely observing residents' experiences with them. It fields a diversely talented team that brings many skills to the initiative, including deep technical ability, management acumen, and market knowledge. It takes a systems approach, simultaneously examining all the elements that must come together to create a working solution to a given problem. It establishes a "leading platform" on which other players—companies, nonprofits, and government agencies—can build technologies and applications.

Practices like these help ensure that HP's investment yields real, sustainable results for the community in question. But HP also sees returns to its own business. In Kuppam, the company is discovering the need for (and developing) new products like a solar-powered digital camera, with printer, that fits in a backpack.

By engaging the community and its leaders and working with them to design valuable new tools and capabilities, HP is gaining the knowledge it needs to be a stronger competitor in other developing regions.

More than a hundred miles from Bangalore, India, the dusty road that runs through Kuppam is bustling with cars, carts, auto rickshaws, and pedestrians. The people from the rural areas surrounding Kuppam often travel for hours to use what's here—to shop, to catch the bus that travels to towns beyond, to access government services and resources.

But the services here are not enough to meet the region's growing challenges: Of the nearly 300,000 people who call the villages around Kuppam home, more than half live below the poverty line. When wage earners can

find work, it's usually as migrant laborers or farmers.
One in three citizens is illiterate, more than 50% of
households have no electricity, and in Andhra Pradesh,
the Indian state where Kuppam is located, more than 4
million children do not attend school. These problems
are compounded by a high rate of AIDS—more than
400,000 residents of Andhra Pradesh, including many
who were among the most able-bodied earners, are HIV
positive.

It's exactly this challenging atmosphere that prompted
Hewlett-Packard to choose Kuppam as one of its first
"i-communities," initiatives where the company creates
public–private partnerships to accelerate economic
development through the application of technology
while simultaneously opening new markets and developing new products and services. By assembling an ecosystem of public and private partners, HP hopes to turn
the Kuppam region into a thriving, self-sustaining economy where greater access to technology permanently
improves literacy, creates income, and provides access to
new markets, government services, education, and health
care. (For a glimpse into that ecosystem, see "An Hour
in the Life of an Information Center" at the end of this
article.)

It's still early in the project's intended three-year life
span—the Kuppam i-community has just celebrated its
first anniversary. (For a description of the project's four
phases, see the exhibit "Making a Sustainable Contribution.") But progress has already been made and much
has been learned. As multinational companies, governments, nongovernmental organizations (NGOs), and
communities join to drive economic and social change in
a variety of nations, the Kuppam i-community project

Making a Sustainable Contribution

The four phases of HP's Kuppam i-community project

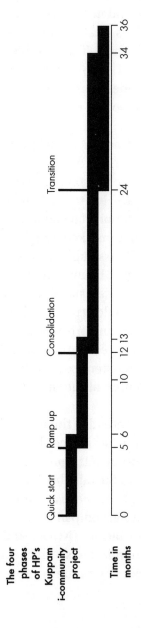

| Quick start | Ramp up | Consolidation | Transition |

Time in months

0   5 6   10   12 13   24   34 36

Quick start

Host conversations with representatives of the full community.

Stage a "visioning" exercise, in which a graphic facilitator depicts the community's ideas and hopes in a rich, vibrant mural; that approach enables broad participation, regardless of language and literacy, and keeps the focus on overarching goals.

Reach agreement on areas that would be well served by enhanced information and communications technology.

Gain high-level alignment with partners in the private and public sectors.

Develop a prioritized list of Web- and other technology-based solutions.

Outline projects to prototype, touching on all of the community's focus areas.

Establish credibility and momentum by achieving some quick successes.

Ramp up

Gather resources required for prototyping.

Create prototypes of Web-based services and solutions in areas such as education, health, and agriculture.

Involve partners and "users" (community members) throughout the process to test the validity of each approach.

Evaluate solutions for their usefulness in the community and their potential for success in other developing markets.

Design and build the necessary communications infrastructure.

Train stakeholders so they can begin to own the initiatives and assume leadership of them.

Turn the ecosystem of global and local partners into a true coalition, with defined expectations and performance metrics for all parties.

Consolidation

Evaluate the intellectual property, relationships, and practices generated to date.

Help local partners decide which solutions to deploy more widely within the community.

Take the best ideas to scale; stop projects that are not likely to reach their goals.

Figure out how to replicate the successful parts of the initiative in other communities.

Transition

Identify leaders in the community.

Transfer power, know-how, and process skills to local participants.

Ensure that the solutions are sustainable without HP's day-to-day involvement.

can serve as a place to test new ways of working and achieving results for communities around the world.

A Better Way to Make a Difference

This i-community project represents a new breed of initiative that fuses HP's global-citizenship strategy and its business strategy. What does that mean? For one thing, it means HP's efforts there do not fall under the heading of philanthropy. Philanthropy is important to Hewlett-Packard, but we at HP want our contribution and involvement in global-citizenship initiatives to have a far greater impact than simply writing a check would.

Consider the impact Hewlett-Packard is having on the lives of two young women in the village of Thodia-lyellagatti. Saraswati and Gowri are both intelligent and energetic, but they had to drop out of school after completing seventh and fifth grade, respectively, because their families could not afford their schooling. Today, both are members of a self-help group in their village that has equivalents in other areas of the country. Members of such groups, almost all of whom are women, put aside small sums of money each week; the pooled money is then available for loans to members. Once a group's assets reach a certain point, the government matches the money for loan-making purposes. Some self-help groups have grown large enough to fund business start-ups, such as food processing and textile companies, that require capital equipment.

When HP decided to pilot a new solar-powered digital camera and printer setup small enough to fit in a back-pack, the company went to the self-help group in Thodi-alyellagatti. The idea was to test the digital photography solution as a vehicle to generate new jobs for Kuppam residents. We wanted to determine what kind of revenue could be generated for holders of the new jobs and find out whether there was a sustainable business model that HP could replicate more broadly. Saraswati and Gowri were among ten women chosen to be trained as village photographers and given free cameras, printers, and other equipment. After two weeks of training, they were able to serve as the official photographers for the debut of the first round of i-community solutions and services at a week-long launch event.

That "solutions week" culminated in an inauguration ceremony presided over by Chandrababu Naidu, the chief minister of Andhra Pradesh. Seeing how people loved having their pictures taken with their elected representative, Saraswati and Gowri seized on a business opportunity: They followed Naidu on his rounds, selling inexpensive photo ops. In the course of just a few days, both women earned the equivalent of a month's income. Today they continue to earn money, if at a less frenetic pace, selling photo IDs. Positioning themselves in front of a government office at peak hours, they are Kuppam's equivalent of an instant-photo booth. They also photograph engagement ceremonies, public works in progress, and a wide variety of other events and scenes that in the past were not documented because photography was too expensive for anything but very special occasions.

For Saraswati and Gowri, the additional source of income will mean a better education for their children, not to mention the prospect of a water tap at home. But the experience has had an even larger impact than that. Recently, the two women were talking excitedly about their upcoming meeting with the manager of a co-op bank; the plan was to discuss a line of credit for their self-help group. This, they said, would not have been conceivable before they had found success as photographers. They would not have had the confidence.

This inspiring story grew out of HP's commitment to what we call "e-inclusion"—using technology to close the economic and social divide as a matter of both global citizenship and business strategy. Taking on citizenship initiatives that make sense in terms of our business strategy means we become a better global competitor in the process. It also means greater social impact, because we can bring HP's business strengths to bear.

Applying Management Practices

One effect of aligning our global-citizenship strategy with our business strategy is that we are applying the rigor and processes of a well-managed company to problems that need to be solved. It's partly an issue of mindset: Because we have clear strategic objectives for the initiative, we approach the project as business managers. It's also a matter of Hewlett-Packard's particular capabilities; we follow certain practices very well. We're employing seven of these practices in Kuppam, as detailed in the following pages.

UNEARTHING CUSTOMER NEEDS

In the technology industry, breakthrough products and services rarely come about as a result of asking customers what they want. Customers are notoriously unable to envision what doesn't exist. Instead, successful companies divine the needs of their customers by probing at underlying problems and transferring that understanding to the innovation process. Few community development initiatives benefit from this line of thinking, however. Perhaps it's because these programs are funded as purely philanthropic endeavors and the relationship between the companies making the donations and the communities being targeted typically depends on an intermediary nonprofit. Whatever the reason, this phase is usually addressed in a cursory manner or bypassed altogether.

From the start, HP has approached the economic and social challenges in Kuppam by investing in a needs-finding process, which features an iterative cycle. When we unearth a need, we rapidly prototype a solution to it. We deploy that solution on a limited basis and closely observe Kuppam residents' experience with it. Based on what we learn, we make modifications, allowing the solution to evolve—then we begin the cycle anew. As a result, each generation of solutions is more sophisticated than the last, and over a short period, solutions become tightly matched to what citizens truly need. It's a methodology we refer to as a "living lab," and it's based on the methods we use in HP Labs to develop new products and technologies. In Kuppam, we've made it possible for local entrepreneurs to build community information centers where residents can tap into on-line government services. As they are rolled out, the centers are refined based on the responses of the citizen-customers.

FIELDING A DIVERSELY TALENTED TEAM

Envisioning a solution tailored to unmet customer needs is only part of the challenge. We also have to scale those solutions to the larger community. That requires a diverse set of talents. Here again, we take what we've learned in business and apply it in the community.

Traditionally, most multinational companies entrust their community-engagement and development initiatives to professionals with backgrounds in philanthropy and development. We know we need to tap such experts, but we also want to see other perspectives and capabilities on the team—like deep business acumen, line-management skills, expertise in government affairs and policy analysis, and a rich understanding of the specific culture in which the initiative will be deployed. The i-community project in Kuppam is led by HP's Emerging Market Solutions team and powered by HP employees from HP Labs, Philanthropy, Education, Government Affairs, and HP's e-inclusion team. The effort also encompasses the local leadership and employees of HP India, along with volunteers there. It's a complicated undertaking to assemble and manage such a diverse team, but we believe this model of engagement is essential for creating maximum economic and social value.

TAKING A SYSTEMS APPROACH

In HP's own reinvention efforts as a company, the leadership team has taken a systems approach—that is, rather than isolate parts of the system and attempt to improve their performance separately, we consider the parts in context and work to optimize the whole. We've framed all of the elements of our business—strategy; structure and process; metrics and rewards; and company culture and behavior—and we are working every aspect simultaneously to drive results. We're taking a similar systems approach in Kuppam, and with a similar frame. We're simultaneously examining the strategy of sustainable development in India; the structure of the team and community to make progress; the metrics that help us assess how we're performing; and the culture we need to instill in the HP i-community team and in the Kuppam community.

The point is that although technology is central to making progress in Kuppam, far more is required to ensure a sustainable contribution. Community leaders must advocate for the solution, trusted individuals within the community must lend their reputations to the effort, Kuppam businesses must get involved, and other technology companies must integrate their technology into the solution. That brings us to another aspect of our approach.

CREATING A LEADING PLATFORM

It's a truism in the information technology industry that to achieve effective solutions, a company must address the full value chain: the set of product and service providers that, taken together, satisfy a customer's need. The best way to serve customers—and therefore to fuel profitable growth—is to design a value chain that will deliver a total solution, not simply provide point solutions. This is not to say that HP believes it should provide the entire value chain on its own. Instead, we work to develop a platform to which partners can add technologies and applications.

In Kuppam, we are similarly finding that there are many benefits to creating a leading platform. The platform we're creating consists of a 2-megabit-per-second network, five community information centers, and online services—health information, literacy programs, information for farmers, assistance to people applying for government programs, and so forth—that we are developing with the government. The platform has succeeded in attracting additional partners and developers. World Links (a global network for the improvement of teaching and learning through the use of information technology), Digital Partners (an organization that links entrepreneurs in the IT realm with social entrepreneurs, foundations, and development institutions), and other for-profit and not-for-profit organizations are now coming to Kuppam to build their own solutions on top of it. We expect that the benefits of HP's initial actions will be greatly multiplied by the organizations that leverage the platform.

BUILDING AN ECOSYSTEM OF PARTNERS

From the get-go, we've structured the initiative to draw on the strengths of the Andhra Pradesh government, Kuppam's municipal leadership, local businesspeople, informal networks within the community, health care professionals, NGOs, local and international technology partners, and the community as a whole. Anyone who has led a large community initiative for a multinational will tell you that this isn't the easiest path to take in the short term. Balancing the interests, work methods, and preferences of the various groups is a challenge. Each participant has its own core motivation, metabolism for change, tolerance for risk, and scorecard for what constitutes success. That's probably why, for all the talk about public–private partnerships, there are still remarkably few examples of highly successful models in developing nations. But we are convinced that, as in the technology industry, the most sustainable communities are those in which many different players have a vested interest in perpetuating a given solution. So instead of attempting

to drive all the value ourselves, we are trying to create a
healthy ecosystem of partners, all dedicated to solving
the problem.

SETTING A DEADLINE

To improve the likelihood of productive results, we
believe it's important for us or for any multinational
corporation to set a time limit for participation in a
community-based project. It's critical to state from the
beginning that your objective is to create a self-sustaining
initiative—and to signal that, you must make clear from
the outset how long you intend to take part in it. (The
Kuppam project, as we've mentioned, is a three-year commitment on the part of HP.) Such a time limit has two
positive effects: First, urgency keeps all the participants in
the partnership focused. Second, it biases the initiatives
toward action, not rhetoric, encouraging participants to
find points of highest common purpose rather than to
focus on the differences between them.

SOLVING, STITCHING, AND SCALING

Finally, we bring to Kuppam the pragmatism that HP has
learned through years of taking generations of new products to market. With a new technology solution, it often
makes sense to focus the first prototype on one high-
profile customer's version of the problem, rather than try
to provide, out of the box, for all the forms the product
will eventually take. Such a first customer is known as a
"lighthouse account" because, if it is well served, the customer will point others toward you. It serves as proof of
concept and a shining example. In Kuppam, we are not

attempting to solve the entire problem from the outset. Instead, we are focusing on solving parts of it well—and, in the process, building a collection of subsolutions. As we make progress, we stitch those together to create a total solution and then take it to scale. That approach isn't unique to Hewlett-Packard in the business world. What distinguishes our method is that we apply our usual pragmatism to global-citizenship initiatives.

Kuppam's Business Value to HP

We've been discussing what HP brings to the table in Kuppam, the organizational approaches and strengths that enable us to be a valuable partner in that community's efforts. But by design, the exchange of value is two way. HP has also been a beneficiary, gaining knowledge and contacts that will make the company a stronger competitor in the global economy.

The Kuppam i-community will lead to new kinds of technology solutions that will prove valuable in India and other areas too. We've already mentioned our project involving solar-powered digital photography. That particular solution—the photo studio in a backpack, as it were, with its potential for creating jobs and income—grew out of conditions and needs observed in Kuppam, where it's simply not realistic to expect that many people would buy PCs, cameras, and color printers for personal use, as they do in the United States. Many of the on-line services we're developing are similarly promising for applications beyond Kuppam. In addition to new products, we are creating intangible assets—like new networks and increased familiarity with new markets—that will have an important impact on our bottom line.

In the process of accomplishing all this, we are also developing world-class leaders. Consider the responsibility that now belongs to HP leader Anand Tawker, who was chosen to lead the i-community effort in India. Marshaling and focusing the talent of diverse groups requires insight, vision, cultural understanding, and business acumen. HP was confident that Tawker would bring strong business-planning skills to the project; he had run several business initiatives at HP and other technology companies. He was fluent in technology development and innovation processes. Perhaps just as important, Tawker, who is of Indian descent, could ensure that Hewlett-Packard would operate in a culturally appropriate way within the i-community. Yet even with all these past successes and capabilities on his side, Tawker says his current post as the director of the Kuppam i-community effort has challenged him. "In so many ways, I think my previous experience was just a prelude to this job," he says. "But in the same breath, I'll tell you that Kuppam pushes me in so many different, unexpected ways—calling on every fiber of what I know so we can invent new things, new solutions, and new ways of working."

The mark of successful companies in our industry is that they can reinvent themselves, and that requires capable, resilient leaders. Living labs like Kuppam offer an unmatched opportunity for managers to develop the skills they need to lead businesses in the twenty-first century. More can be learned in three years in a living lab than in virtually any leadership-development program or graduate course. Indeed, though it wasn't among the primary goals of the i-community, teaching leaders new ways to lead may be one of the largest competitive benefits of the initiative. Ultimately, it's the knowledge that these leaders and their teams gain in places like Kuppam that will allow HP to become a stronger competitor.

A New Framework for Global Engagement

Fusing our global-citizenship and business strategy is about doing good and doing well in the same activities—as opposed to doing well in order to do good. This hasn't been our traditional approach. Certainly, like many multinational companies, HP has a history of philanthropic efforts. In 1939, founders Bill Hewlett and Dave Packard donated a portion of their first year's profits to local causes. In the years since, HP has contributed more than $1 billion in gifts, in-kind donations, and time to causes around the world. A few years ago, however, we realized that while our philanthropic efforts were generating results, the results were suboptimal. We saw that we could achieve much more if doing good and doing well were mutually reinforcing (and with recent world events, we felt we *needed* to be doing more). At the same time, we thought we could achieve more for HP's business in the process—a vital consideration for our shareholders as well as for our competitiveness.

This is why we developed the HP Global Citizenship Framework. (See the exhibit "A Focus for Global Citizenship Efforts.") We wanted to map out and clearly communicate our priorities in this area and help our organizations align around this new way of thinking.

The Kuppam i-community initiative demonstrates our commitment to e-inclusion and community engagement and makes a great deal of business sense for Hewlett-Packard. As a high-priority growth market for HP, India has many potential customers for new HP technologies, products, and solutions. We also chose

A Focus for Global Citizenship Efforts

What does it mean to be a good global citizen? At Hewlett-Packard, we now use a simple framework to answer that question. At its core are values that must never change. Strong ethics and appropriately transparent governance form the platform of integrity on which all our policies and decisions must be based. And deep engagement with key stakeholders in the communities where we do business is essential to ensuring a positive impact.

More particular to our industry and the current moment are the three burning issues we're focused on: privacy, the environment, and "e-inclusion" (which has a strong component of education). Regarding privacy rights, we were the first company in the Fortune 50 to join Safe Harbor, the international data-protection agreement outlining rules for transfer of consumer data across international borders. On the environmental front, we have an explicit goal of designing new products so as to minimize their ecological impact, from production through disposal. Our e-inclusion and education program focuses on using technology to give people access to social and economic opportunities. Our goal is not simply to participate, but to be a leader, in each of these areas.

Finally, the outer edge of the framework highlights three key competencies or assets that we deploy. We work with the U.S. government and governments around the world to shape and influence policy. We make philanthropic contributions of funds and resources. And we communicate broadly, to raise consciousness of the problems we see and to increase awareness of effective solutions.

Deceptively simple, the framework reflects many long hours of complex analysis and discussion. It allows us to easily communicate the new strategy to employees and partners so that they can align their actions with ours.

Kuppam because of what it could help HP learn about nascent or "white space" opportunities—the high-potential opportunities that lie between markets or outside HP's current focus areas. We believe HP's richest opportunities and best chances for innovation lie in regions that rank user and organizational needs very differently from the way established markets and customers do. Finally, Kuppam is a community on the move, led by a particularly ambitious network of government officials, business owners, and social leaders who want to create change for the citizens of the region. In fact, it was because Kuppam has such strong, willing leadership— and the fundamental institutions required to support change—that HP chose to put its first i-community project there.

No question: We are placing the highest priority on communities where we can "engage the engageable." In Kuppam's case, Chandrababu Naidu, the chief minister of Andhra Pradesh, has a powerful vision for his constituents, and the use of information technology is central to that vision. Among his other goals is achieving a 100% literacy rate within a three-year period. Naidu and his team have played an active role in selecting community leaders in Kuppam to anchor various parts of the initiative.

A multinational corporation is not a government—we are always mindful of that. We know we can have an impact only if there's a base level of functioning systems, institutions, and programs. Change is not possible until there is a capable network to support it. When global-citizenship efforts and business efforts are being fused, it's important to choose initiatives based on the strength of local leadership. Naidu will take full advantage of the i-community to improve the effectiveness and reach of government services, use technology to disseminate information about public health, and use the pilot project to generate new jobs and economic opportunities. We picked Kuppam because we knew HP could be a catalyzing force for his initiatives.

The Long View

Kuppam's i-community now encompasses five physical community information centers—with more on the way—where students, teachers, parents, and others can learn skills and get access to information and services via the Internet. It features a government portal—usable from any Web-enabled device—that gives Kuppam residents access to government Web sites and services. The i-community also features a mobile service center with wireless access and new technology-empowered social programs such as Naidu's literacy program. These are the kinds of tools Kuppam needs to unleash its talents and ambitions. The journey of the next two years is to scale these nascent solutions to meet the needs of the full community.

But we are already hearing that Kuppam's people are thinking inventively to improve their lives. There's the self-help group that is beginning to use computers to track the performance metrics that enable members to qualify for financial aid and government services; they'll no longer have to rely on complicated ledger systems that require specialized bookkeepers. There's the village photographer helping farmers by transmitting snapshots of crop pests to distant experts who can advise on how to control the damage. There are stories of parents using a Web-based service to find the basic health information they need to care for their children.

The results of this living-lab approach are specific solutions that meet the needs of the Kuppam community. But more than that, the solutions are proof of an approach that we believe will unearth ways to solve the needs of governments, businesses, communities, and individuals in emerging markets in other areas of the world.

These are the kinds of projects that corporations must collectively embark on—weak economy or no. They are not about short-term profits but about the opportunity of achieving long-term growth and, in the process, fundamentally improving the human condition in the regions where companies do business.

An Hour in the Life of an Information Center

THE COMMUNITY INFORMATION CENTER in Kuppam is located downtown, a stone's throw from the main bus terminal. Surrounded by houses, fruit sellers with pushcarts, and stalls and stores offering utensils, bangles, and flowers, it's in the heart of the central bazaar. Its large sign features the yellow and red "PCO" that is ubiquitous in the Indian landscape today, indicating that it's a public call office—people can go there to make phone calls. The sign also announces that customers can make photocopies and use various communication services, such as faxes.

A narrow flight of stairs leads to a 400-square-foot office with a neat line of four workstations, each housing one computer. Users can obtain information about services and programs by using the computers to access the HP-built i-community portal.

Uma Rani, the 25-year-old high school graduate who is one of the three co-owners of this CIC, is on-site this morning. She and two other first-time entrepreneurs were chosen after a rigorous selection process by World Corps, an organization whose mission is to generate employment in developing countries. The three joined forces for the first time in starting this venture, which is funded by a loan offered under the auspices of the chief minister's Employment of Youth program. Hewlett-Packard provided much of the equipment in the center and designed many of the Web-based services on the i-community portal that can be accessed at the CIC.

Chelliah is a typical walk-in customer. This 65-year-old native of the adjoining village of Kankundi retired a year ago after serving as the headmaster of the only school in his village. He is visiting Kuppam to follow up on a petition he presented to the government regarding his land records. He needs to photocopy documents that have to be submitted. As Uma Rani begins the copying, she strikes up a conversation with Chelliah about his family and life in Kankundi. She also takes a moment to apprise him of new services he can apply for at the CIC via the HP i-community portal. She asks if he has heard of the government's program for retired teachers. He hasn't. After getting a little more information from him, Uma Rani is able to print out a list of programs he might avail himself of.

Before Chelliah has left, an application for the program for retired teachers has been submitted electronically and acknowledgement of the submission has been received. The application for the benefits will have to be approved at the district level; he can expect to have a response within a week. Uma Rani informs him that, as it happens, her partner Suresh will be in Chelliah's village the following week, leading a team of high school students reading electricity meters after school hours. Uma Rani will ask Suresh to pass on the word about the application's outcome.

Meanwhile, in the station next to Uma Rani's, her other partner, Krishna, is handing a check to Lakshmiamma,a pregnant woman. Lakshmiamma's scenario was similar to Chelliah's in some ways: She had happened into the CIC last week to make a phone call while visiting Kuppam for her monthly checkup at a hospital. She is entitled to benefits through a government program aimed at helping pregnant women below the poverty line. But she had not even known that such a scheme existed—until she walked into the CIC.

Originally published in August 2003
Reprint R0308C

Abraham Lincoln and the Global Economy

ROBERT D. HORMATS

Executive Summary

ABRAHAM LINCOLN WOULD HAVE well understood the challenges facing many modern emerging nations. In Lincoln's America, as in many developing nations today, sweeping economic change threatened older industries, traditional ways of living, and social and national cohesion by exposing economies and societies to new and powerful competitive forces.

Yet even in the midst of the brutal and expensive American Civil War—and in part because of it—Lincoln and the Republican Congress enacted bold legislation that helped create a huge national market, a strong and unified economy governed by national institutions, and a rising middle class of businessmen and property owners.

Figuring out how to maximize the benefits of globalization while minimizing its disruptions is a formidable

23

challenge for policy makers. How do you expand opportunities for the talented and the lucky while making sure the rest of society doesn't fall behind? It may be helpful to look at the principles that informed the policies that Lincoln and the Republican Congress instituted after they came to power in 1861:

- Facilitate the upward mobility of low- and middle-income groups to give them a significant stake in the country.

- Emphasize the good of the national economy over regional interests.

- Affirm the need for sound government institutions to temper the dynamics of the free enterprise system.

- Tailor policies to the national situation.

- Realize that a period of turmoil may present a unique opportunity for reform.

These principles drove the reforms that helped Americans cope with and benefit from rapid technological advances and the fast integration of the American economy in the nineteenth century. They may be instructive to today's policy makers who are struggling to help their own citizens integrate into the fast-changing global economy of the twenty-first century.

ON A SPRING NIGHT IN 1856, the side-wheel steamboat *Effie Afton* crashed into a railroad bridge spanning the Mississippi River between Davenport, Iowa, and Rock Island, Illinois. The ship burned and sank.

This wasn't the first such mishap: Since the construction of this, the first railroad bridge across the Mississippi, captains unfamiliar with the man-made obstacle had banged into it many times. Claiming that the bridge was hazardous to navigation, the boat's owners sued the Rock Island Bridge Company for damages.

More was at play here than safety. It was clear that rail traffic across the Mississippi could become an increasingly formidable competitor to river traffic. For boat owners, this was a chance to slow the growth of a challenger, if not stop it entirely. Indeed, the bridge owners were concerned not only about the suit but also about demands by shipping and port interests that the structure—itself seriously damaged in the collision—be torn down and new bridges be banned altogether.

To defend them in court, the bridge owners wanted someone who knew both railroads and riverboats. They decided on an up-and-coming lawyer with a fair amount of experience in railroad litigation, a former one-term Whig congressman who had once been a river boatman himself. His name was Abraham Lincoln.

This 150-year-old legal case would seem to have little bearing on today's global economy. But embedded in it—and in Lincoln's arguments on behalf of the Rock Island Bridge Company—are many of the same tensions and conflicting economic forces confronting today's emerging nations. How Lincoln handled the conflict between entrenched interests rooted in the past and the imperatives of the coming new economic order holds surprisingly relevant lessons for today's international policy makers.

A Nation in Turmoil

It's commonplace to say that we live in a period of unprecedented change. But in the view of many historians, the America of Lincoln was a time of changes at least as jarring.

The country entered the nineteenth century with a predominantly agricultural economy, composed largely of scattered rural communities. Then, in quick succession, steamboat service was introduced, scores of canals were constructed, thousands of miles of railroad track were laid, and countless new telegraph lines were strung throughout the country.

Almost overnight, large numbers of what had been generally self-sufficient local economies found themselves, ready or not, part of a relentlessly changing and expanding national economy. Competition no longer came from the next town but from producers in many parts of the country—and from industries abroad. People traveled farther and more often. New technologies also changed the workplace, as Americans used to laboring for themselves or in small shops began to take jobs in the nation's growing number of factories. The rise of factory-based mass production and frenetic railway construction led to an economic boom. But the nation's growth was interrupted by financial crises—known at the time as panics—in 1819, 1837, and 1857. These produced sharp increases in unemployment, large numbers of bankruptcies and farm foreclosures, and frequent runs on banks.

Not surprisingly, many antebellum Americans resented the developments that led to this volatility, whatever the long-term economic benefits. Most Americans still thought of themselves primarily as residents of their own states—which were often referred to as "countries"—rather than as citizens of a wider American nation. To many, the erosion of the economic boundaries separating communities and states, and the increasing competition from other regions, came as a shock.

Foreign competition, too, threatened jobs and social stability. In Northern states, where the products of newly established steel and machinery-manufacturing plants had to compete with European imports, protectionist pressures were strong. Except for slavery, the subject of trade and tariff levels was the most regionally divisive topic in American politics during the nineteenth century. The growth of manufacturing led to complaints that workers were being exploited. Many saw "wage slavery"—as opposed to self-employment—as antithetical to the principles of freedom and independence on which the country was founded. Protests also arose over widening income inequality, as some sectors of the economy expanded much faster than others, and those who invested or worked in the fastest-growing areas or industries reaped large gains. Enormous tensions built up between those who could benefit from the economic changes and those who felt threatened by them.

Some of these tensions were reflected in the *Effie Afton* case. Lincoln, relying upon his own experience on the Mississippi and a firsthand examination of the site, argued that the boat's pilot could have avoided the accident if he had paid more attention to the currents. (There had even been whispers that the *Effie Afton* had intentionally rammed the bridge with the aim of destroying it.) But Lincoln also addressed broader issues, criticizing those who were using the case as a way to halt or reverse the economic progress ushered in by the railway. He was all in favor of expanding Mississippi River traffic, he said. But, with the arrival of the railroad, "there is a travel from East to West, whose demands are not less important than that of the river. It is growing larger and larger, building up new countries"—even Lincoln used this colloquial term for states—"with a rapidity never before seen in the history of the world."

Lincoln's defense of the bridge company—which was ultimately successful when the jury was unable to deliver a verdict—not only reflected the issues and tensions of the time but also highlighted one of Lincoln's own interests: bolstering the national economy through the development of the American West. Clearly, Lincoln's extraordinary role in history lies in his preservation of the Union and abolition of slavery. But his preoccupation in the early years of his political career, well before he became engaged in the antislavery fight, was the development of the U.S. economy. And the success he and Republican legislators enjoyed in the election of 1860 was due in large part to their economic policies. These included government support for expansion of the nation's railroad network and for homestead laws that gave Eastern factory workers and farmers the opportunity to settle Western lands. In fact, the Republicans' economic platform served as a sweetener to substantial portions of the electorate that were largely ambivalent about the party's antislavery views.

Taken as a whole, the policies were designed to cope with, and expand the benefits of, the tumultuous technological and economic changes that were shaking America. The successful implementation of those plans—achieved in the midst of the most disruptive event in the country's history, the Civil War—contributed to the creation of a huge national market, a strong and unified economy governed by national institutions, and a rising middle class of businessmen and property owners. These together helped transform a rural and developing country into a more modern and prosperous nation—the precursor of the America we know today.

Lessons for the Global Economy

Lincoln would have well understood the challenges facing many modern emerging nations, particularly large and diverse ones such as China, Russia, India, Brazil, and Indonesia. Of course, the context is different. Today, the forces of economic disruption are generally external rather than internal. The source of turmoil is the rapid expansion of international commerce, finance, communications, and transportation, which is inexorably drawing industrialized and emerging nations together into one large global economy.

But many of the consequences of globalization are the same as those known to nineteenth-century Americans. Today, as then, sweeping economic change threatens older industries, traditional ways of living, and social and national cohesion by exposing economies and societies to new and powerful competitive forces. Emerging nations and former Communist countries, once only loosely connected to the global commercial and financial system, feel the shock waves of periodic economic crises resulting from the rapid exodus of foreign capital and sudden adverse shifts in international trade flows, which lead to large numbers of lost jobs and bankruptcies. Some individuals, groups, and regions initially benefit greatly from expanded opportunity—from the ability to sell more abroad, work for foreign companies in their own countries and overseas, or obtain foreign capital for their businesses. Others, however, usually the least educated and least skilled, feel left behind and disfranchised.

Now, as then, we also hear charges of worker exploitation, this time because multinationals have established manufacturing facilities in low-wage countries. And, in another echo of Lincoln's time, there are calls for protectionist measures. These come not only from companies and workers in industrialized countries, who must compete with lower-priced goods from emerging economies, but also from companies and workers in emerging economies, who must compete against the industrialized economies' more technologically advanced products.

Figuring out how to maximize the benefits of globalization—the potential to increase exports, spawn a new generation of entrepreneurs, and attract foreign investment—while minimizing its disruptions is a formidable challenge for policy makers. Many people in emerging nations have the skills, the agility, the resources, and the entrepreneurial capacity to take advantage of new opportunities; many others, probably a significant majority at the outset, do not. How do you expand opportunities for the former—and include in that group more than the political elite and the well educated—while supporting the latter, so they don't fall further behind and become alienated from society?

One could benefit by looking to Lincoln and the Republican Congress that came to power with him after the election of 1860. Emerging economies today are unlikely to replicate their policies per se. But much can be learned from the principles that informed those policies:

- Facilitate the upward mobility of low- and middle-income groups—and give them a significant stake in their country—by increasing their opportunity to own property and establish businesses.

- Emphasize the good of the national economy over regional interests.

- Affirm a role for government—and the need for sound government institutions—to support the economic and technological changes that emerge from the dynamics of the free enterprise system.

- Tailor your policies to your own national situation.

- Realize that a period of turmoil, while potentially a barrier to reform, may also present a unique opportunity.

These principles drove the reforms that helped Americans cope with and benefit from rapid technological change and the fast integration of the American economy in the nineteenth century. They may be instructive to contemporary policy makers in Beijing, Moscow, New Delhi, Brasilia, Jakarta, and elsewhere who struggle to help their own citizens in the fast-changing, rapidly integrating global economy of the twenty-first century.

Economic Opportunity for All

Lincoln believed in the American dream. After all, he was a living exemplar of it. "I am not ashamed to confess that 25 years ago I was a hired laborer, mauling rails, at work on a flatboat—just what might happen to any poor man's son," he once said. And he had great faith in the abilities of others to realize that dream, if given the chance: "The prudent, penniless beginner in the world labors for wages awhile, saves a surplus with which to buy tools or land for himself, then labors on his own account another while, and at length hires another new beginner to help him."

To Lincoln, the promise of upward mobility was key both to the nation's economic growth and to its social stability. It was in the churning energy and desire of Americans, their quest to improve their lives, that Lincoln saw the great promise for the country. Government's role was to ensure that they had the opportunity to succeed in this quest. He flatly rejected the popular notion that society needed a permanent class of low-wage workers to provide the foundation for economic progress—an idea that in its most extreme form was the rationale for slavery. The cornerstone of his policy was the concept of "free labor"—the notion that all Americans, whites and blacks alike, deserve the chance to advance in life. Indeed, just as Lincoln argued that America could not sustain itself as a nation half slave and half free, so he also believed that it could not sustain itself 5% rich and 95% poor.

Without sufficient opportunity for lower- and middle-class Americans to get ahead, Lincoln feared, the country would suffer from the kind of divisive class warfare that was spreading in Europe. Even in America, political and social unrest was growing, the result of widening income inequality between rich and poor. (By 1863, the top 1% of New Yorkers held 61% of the city's wealth.) Steps needed to be taken to ensure that a large portion of society—including the increasing number of immigrants coming in search of new opportunities—didn't feel that the road to prosperity was blocked.

Lincoln made no apology for the fact that economic development would initially benefit some Americans and not others. The wage premium for skilled workers on the railroads and in the new factories was high, fueling resentment among less-skilled workers. But the fact that many of these unskilled workers lived in squalid conditions with little immediate hope of improving their lives didn't undermine Lincoln's belief that they had the potential for upward mobility—or if not, that their children did. For this reason, he rejected outright the idea that Northern factory workers were worse off than Southern slaves because, in the words of one Southern politician, slaves were "hired for life and well compensated" while manual laborers were "hired by the day, not cared for, and scantily compensated."

Lincoln and his Republican Party—like the Whig Party to which he had previously belonged—believed that free-market capitalism was the best way to create economic opportunity. But Lincoln did not believe in a laissez-faire approach; he favored proactive policies to achieve this goal. One such policy was promoting property ownership. The opening up of the American West, already viewed as a key to the nation's economic growth (recall Lincoln's passionate arguments in the *Effie Afton* case), presented an opportunity to further this aim. The Homestead Act, passed by Lincoln's Republican Congress, not only offered settlers 160-acre parcels of land but also established a single uniform national system for granting them clear title to it. The program was in line with Lincoln's belief that "it is best for all to leave each man free to acquire property as fast as he can."

Congress and the Lincoln administration also took into account the economic interests of lower- and middle-income Americans through radical tax reform. Before the Civil War, the federal government had depended on tariffs for more than 90% of its revenue, with land sales accounting for most of the rest. But the enormous cost of the war required other sources of income. So, in the face of bitter opposition from wealthy Americans, among others, Congress passed legislation imposing a federal income tax. Even more controversial, the tax rate was progressive, although modestly so by today's standards. The tax rate initially was set at a uniform 3% of annual income, but people below a certain income—and that included most wage earners—weren't required to pay the tax at all. Later legislation required wealthier Americans to pay at a 5% rate, and then a 10% rate, with lower brackets for lower income groups. Although the Civil War income tax was abolished in

1872, the precedent had been set for today's progressive tax system.

Finally, Congress sought to enhance educational opportunities. It passed legislation granting federal lands for "institutions of agricultural and mechanical instruction"; in many cases, these quickly became general universities. The legislation also encouraged the admission of women to state universities. One of the most progressive pieces of legislation passed in the nineteenth century, this act broadened educational opportunities in Western states and ultimately throughout the nation, thus reinforcing the role of government in promoting upward mobility.

Over time, the Lincoln administration's policies helped many Americans to markedly improve their standard of living. Although they didn't eliminate the enormous wage disparities between the very rich and the very poor that became the focus of social reformers in the early twentieth century, they did foster a sense of well-being and dignity among the growing middle class of property owners. This enabled the United States to resist the worst aspects of class warfare that broke out in Europe at the turn of the twentieth century and the destabilizing and repressive collectivist movements— socialism, communism, and fascism—that arose in response to this strife.

What lessons do Lincoln's upward mobility policies hold for today's emerging economies? A major charge against globalization today was also leveled against the rapidly integrating American economy of the 1800s: that the educated elite and skilled professionals improve their situation while the vast majority see little immediate benefit and often feel marginalized. This makes Lincoln's pro-opportunity agenda, which laid the foundation for

future American economic and political stability, worthy
of consideration by developing nations. America's experience suggests that initial increases in income inequality need not cause policy makers in emerging economies
undue concern, provided they have a plan in the medium
term to narrow the gap. Of course, not every nation has a
vast frontier that allows for a program like America's
Homestead Act. But even legislation that grants people
clear title to land they now occupy can go a long way
toward fostering the stability inherent in a large
property-owning class.

As for tax policy, the important lesson from the
American experience is that revenue should be generated in ways that are visibly fair but don't stifle growth or
entrepreneurial ambition. Emerging-economy governments have too often erred on one side or the other of
this balance: Some have pursued social goals through
unrealistically high taxation on the wealthy and on business, thereby driving investment away; others have let
ruling elites get away essentially untaxed, often by wink-
ing at corruption and tax evasion. The institution of a
progressive income tax—but with the highest tax
bracket kept at a modest level—was critical to the Lincoln administration's ability to raise revenues needed to
sustain the war effort in a way that was seen as socially
equitable but did not impede capital formation or
growth. Indeed, investment—not only in railroads but
also in factories of all sorts—boomed during this period.

A Unified National Economy

Reducing the threat of class warfare wasn't enough to
ensure political and social stability. Without a robust
national infrastructure and cohesive national economic

institutions, Lincoln believed, the country would suffer from worrisome regional divisions—divisions that would last well beyond the Civil War and would divide Northern states as well.

Before the war, states were discrete and powerful political and economic units. Regional jealousies—not just between the North and the South but also between the urban East and the rural West—were strong. States in one part of the country frequently attempted to block federal financing of a canal or a harbor in another part on the grounds that it did not benefit them. Lincoln fought such parochialism. In a speech made long before he became president, he cited the benefits of the recently completed Illinois and Michigan Canal. It ran entirely within Illinois. But because of it, sugar, for example, could be carried from New Orleans to Buffalo, New York, more cheaply than along the old coastal route. This benefited both the merchants of New Orleans and the people of Buffalo, who, in Lincoln's words, "sweetened their coffee a little more cheaply than before."

To Republicans, such infrastructure projects—known at the time as "internal improvements"—were vital to America's economic development and were an important way to bind the nation together, both physically and psychologically. They fostered interstate commerce, allowing Western farmers to send their products to burgeoning Eastern markets, and Eastern factories to send their goods to the booming West. They promoted geographic mobility, letting more Americans move to, and prosper on, the frontier.

The most notable project championed by the Lincoln administration was the first transcontinental railroad. The Republican Party committed itself to this project in its 1860 platform; Congress authorized it in the Pacific

Railway Act of 1862. That legislation gave developers generous rights of way, large amounts of additional land on each side of the track, and hefty subsidies. This and other legislation helped to nearly double the miles of railroad track in the nation in the ten years between 1860 and 1870, a period dominated by the traumatic events of the Civil War. In 1869, the Union Pacific and Central Pacific lines were joined, connecting the continent.

Most emerging economies today face regional rivalries like those of Lincoln's America. Many of these contemporary divisions are sharpened by intense ethnic rivalries. Still, the gradual transformation of the United States from a collection of states into a nation, in part through the creation of a national transportation infrastructure, can serve as an inspiration to modern countries.

If there is a caveat to the extraordinary expansion of America's railroad network, it involves the absence of regulation to accompany the government's generous support for the railroads. The railroads successfully resisted—in court and in Congress—curbs on their growing economic power. The resulting unregulated competition led to overbuilding, stock market crashes, corruption, and ultimately an oligopolistic industry. For the leaders of emerging economies, the American experience with railroads is a good lesson in the dangers of providing government support for an industry without also putting in place sufficient or effective regulation.

An Active Government Role

Supporting the formation of a national railroad infrastructure wasn't the only way Lincoln fostered national cohesion. His administration also established national financial institutions to reduce economic instability and help Americans take advantage of a nationwide market-place. But unlike in the railroad industry, the federal government imposed regulations on an undisciplined banking industry that had frequently contributed to, and had often caused, disruptive swings in the economy. Most Americans were deeply distrustful of concentrating a lot of power in the federal government and giving it a significant role in managing the economy. At the time, there was no central bank, like today's Federal Reserve, to control the money supply and regulate the banking system. A hodgepodge of state-chartered banks, varying in size and quality, issued notes backed by their own assets and operated with little oversight. Frequent runs on banks and periods of erratic expansion and contraction of bank credit triggered violent booms and busts. Often banknotes lost much or all of their value if the bank collapsed, or excessive credit creation led to rampant inflation. Particularly for Americans who lived in the West, South, and other rural areas, Eastern banks were threatening and alien institutions.

Many banks also were closely connected to local politicians and engaged in what today is called crony capitalism. Lincoln was particularly sensitive to this problem. "Nothing," he said, "is better calculated to engender heartburnings and to enlist enemies of the most hostile character against a bank than for the community to entertain the belief that the institution is used for the benefit of the few to the exclusion of the many."

One possible response to such failings was the revival of a national bank, a permanent successor to two temporary institutions that had been created earlier in the country's history. Such an institution would maintain a stable currency and an adequate money supply. But populist resistance to the concentration of so much financial power in one institution torpedoed the idea.

So the administration pursued the same end by a different means, successfully pushing for legislation that created a decentralized but federally regulated national banking system. Individual banks, located in various parts of the country, were chartered as national banks and authorized by the federal government to issue banknotes. To obtain this privilege, they first had to buy federal government bonds from the Treasury. These bonds secured the notes the banks were empowered to issue. This move pumped needed money into the overall economy—not just in the industrial East. The national banks were subject to federal inspection by the newly established office of the Comptroller of the Currency, resulting in institutions that were generally better managed than the state-chartered banks.

In another bold move, Congress passed legislation authorizing the Treasury to issue its own notes. Those notes, printed on green paper to distinguish them from private banknotes (usually printed on white paper), came to be known as "greenbacks." They were the first paper currency issued directly by the federal government. Creation of the U.S. Federal Reserve was, of course, not to come until 1913. But the dramatic currency and banking reforms of the 1860s—the establishment of a single, uniform currency and a better-regulated national banking system—went a long way toward creating an integrated national economy, making it much easier for American businesses and financiers to operate across the nation.

Today's critics of globalization point to financial crises—the Mexican financial crisis of 1994, for instance, or the Asian crisis of 1997—as signs that the existing system isn't working. They charge that volatile inflows and outflows of money disrupt emerging economies, causing dramatic booms, which benefit the rich, and mighty

busts, which hurt the poor. They vilify the financial institutions, international as well as domestic.

But again, as in Lincoln's time, the solution is effective
reform and regulation. While each emerging nation will
need to establish its own priorities and methods for bank
reform, the fundamental principles of America's reforms
in the 1860s hold a few simple but useful lessons. A
poorly regulated and fragmented banking system leaves
the entire economy vulnerable to crisis. If banks, or the
overall banking system, are perceived to be run for the
benefit of insiders and thus inimical to the interests of
large numbers of citizens, they become targets of domestic resentment. And strong national institutions are
needed to resist the centrifugal tendency of states and
provinces to establish their own financial regulations or
reinterpret national regulations in response to local
political pressures.

Policies to Fit the Place

A central element of the Republicans' economic policy
was something almost universally reviled by economists
today: protectionist tariffs. While Lincoln strove to promote interstate commerce by removing economic barriers between regions, he was a long-standing opponent of
unrestricted free trade with other nations—a philosophy
that was at the time gaining support in Europe and
embraced in much of the South. Tariffs, he and his fellow
Republicans believed, were necessary to protect the
nation's infant industrial sector from foreign competition. In an ironic reversal of more recent political positions, the Democrats, then primarily a party of the South,
generally opposed high tariffs because they inflated the
prices farmers and plantation owners had to pay for

machinery imported from Europe or purchased from America's protected manufacturers in the North. And the South needed to export its cotton, so it did not want to give Europeans an excuse to erect high tariff walls of their own. Who knows if Lincoln would support protectionist policies for emerging nations in today's quite different environment. He might ultimately agree with his Democratic contemporary, William Cullen Bryant, "that competition with foreign producers would stimulate the growth and progress of American firms, while protection would only encourage sluggishness." But Lincoln's position on tariffs illustrates his belief that a nation must tailor its policies to its own political, economic, and social circumstances rather than automatically implement imported or academic models.

Had there been a World Bank in the 1850s to promote large infrastructure projects, or an International Monetary Fund to insist that the United States create a strong central bank, the advice would have been bitterly resisted by many Americans. Such developments had to emerge from domestic political decisions that grew out of many years of debate among competing domestic constituencies and political philosophies.

Similarly, attempts from abroad to force through domestic policy changes on today's emerging economies create enormous resistance and backlash. For example, the consensus formed by the IMF and the World Bank in the 1990s favoring the rapid introduction of market-opening reforms in emerging economies has recently encountered strong opposition. Many in developing countries feel that opening up their economies to foreign capital and competition too quickly has rendered their countries vulnerable to substantial economic and social disruptions before they had time to develop the domestic institutions and the social and geographical cohesion needed to cope with those dislocations. Critics of the rapid opening of economies point to the success of emerging economies like South Korea and Taiwan, which for years maintained high levels of protection and government support for domestic industries—policies that closely resemble those of the Lincoln administration.

If he were here today, Lincoln would undoubtedly caution international policy makers and institutions about imposing doctrinaire policies on emerging economies—and possibly even encourage those nations to resist such attempts. At the same time, he would argue forcefully that these countries themselves should establish robust domestic economic institutions to cope with changing circumstances and not give in to those who resist domestically driven promarket reforms.

Opportunity Amid Turmoil

The Civil War presented an unusual opportunity for Lincoln and congressional Republicans to make sweeping changes in America's economic institutions. For much of the nineteenth century, powerful Southerners in Congress had blocked economic legislation of the kind Lincoln and his Whig and Republican colleagues promoted. The resistance partly resulted from Southern fears about expanding free labor in Western states. It also stemmed from the agrarian South's resistance to policies that would help the "new economy" of the North, with its strong banking and manufacturing interests.

But, as I've noted, opposition also reflected genuine philosophical differences over the proper role of the federal government in the economy. Democrats of the time generally favored a small economic role for Washington, arguing that the Constitution granted the government only limited power to legislate in such areas as infrastructure improvements and banking. The Whigs and later the Republicans argued that the Constitution allowed for more extensive economic legislation and a greater economic role for government. Then, Southern legislators left the Congress as 11 Southern states seceded from the Union. That left a Republican in the White House and a Republican majority in Congress. Secession effectively removed obstacles to the passage of economic legislation that Lincoln's party favored. In fact, the first year of the Lincoln administration has been compared to the first hundred days of Franklin Roosevelt's New Deal in the scope of the reforms accomplished and in the way it reshaped the relationship between the federal government and the economy.

The demands of the Civil War—bloody, expensive, and protracted—easily could have postponed the Republicans' economic agenda. Just after Lincoln took office, fear of war produced another run on the banks, and the Treasury could not pay its bills. Yet despite the turmoil, the administration and Congress instituted the series of dramatic reforms that greatly expanded economic opportunity for millions of Americans and strengthened considerably the economic cohesion and financial institutions of the country. The crisis energized the reformers. The very fluidity of the situation permitted America's leaders to drive the reform process forward against entrenched interests. The need to strengthen the fabric of the American society and economy in light of disruptive forces created the sense of urgency required to enact and implement these reforms very quickly.

Lincoln's personal role in many of these changes was limited. His preoccupation with the war meant that he had to turn much of the day-to-day responsibility for economic governance over to his treasury secretary and to fellow Republicans in Congress. He did so recognizing that his mandates and philosophies were virtually the same as theirs.

Lincoln certainly would reject the argument of many in emerging economies today that, because they face political or economic difficulties at home or abroad, they can't be expected to implement bold reforms. He undoubtedly would reject the notion, proffered by some leaders in the Arab world, for example, that their poor economic performance and lack of market and education reform can be blamed on the prolonged period of tensions with Israel.

Quite the contrary: The current period of political turmoil in Iraq and the Middle East in general could present an opportunity remarkably similar to the one Lincoln seized. In the view of some analysts, many of the region's problems stem from the absence of a progressive education system, heavy layers of government intervention that discourage entrepreneurialism, and the domination of economies by a small elite. The sense of urgency should be at least as acute in the twenty-first century Middle East as it was in nineteenth-century America. Most of its economies have fallen behind those of many other emerging nations. Internal divisions in these countries are only likely to grow if these nations do not prosper and if greater numbers of their people do not perceive a larger stake in, and the opportunity to benefit from, that prosperity.

Emerging Economies Across the Years

Abraham Lincoln inherited a country riddled with internal conflict—not only between North and South but also between cities and rural areas, Eastern states and frontier states, workers and industrialists, and advocates and opponents of a greater role for government in the economy. His aim in trying to create a unified national economy was to reduce disparities and convince Americans that their common good depended on the cooperation of social groups and regions that had perceived their interests to be in conflict.

The relevance of these ideas to today's world makes it tempting to extend certain analogies too far. For symmetry's sake, it might be nice to argue that given the tremendous economic growth of the United States over the past 150 years, today's world should adopt at a global level the kinds of policies and institutions Lincoln and his colleagues adopted at a national level. But Lincoln's economic principles are relevant today not because they provide a framework for an elaborate new economic governance structure for the world. They're relevant because they can help emerging economies seek a path toward integration into the rapidly changing global market economy. In fact, in some ways, today's developing nations are analogous not just to the United States of Lincoln's time but to the individual states as well. They are like the United States in their need to build a robust and cohesive national economy with a strong federal role and increased opportunity for all economic strata. But they are like the states in their need to integrate into a larger economy—in this case a global one—and to reap the fruits of being part of it.

The IMF, the World Bank, the World Trade Organization, and other international institutions would do well to consider the lessons of Lincoln's economic policies. Their advice, along with that of industrialized nations, has an important influence on the development agenda for emerging economies. But Lincoln's policies are particularly relevant to leaders and policy makers in the emerging nations themselves. President Putin in Moscow, President "Lula" in Brasilia, and President Hu in Beijing face many of the same issues President Lincoln faced. They each govern a big and diverse country, with a rapidly changing economy. They confront powerful regional disparities and economic divisions. Their banking systems are relatively weak, and their economic institutions are often untested and evolving. Powerful groups demand more opportunity and less government interference in their quest to benefit from the forces of change, while other groups, no less powerful, demand more government support and protection from those same forces. The threats of class warfare and regional disaffection are never far away. In responding to such challenges, these leaders may draw insights from their own countries' histories or from the experiences of today's other emerging economies—or, somewhat surprisingly, from the experience of Abraham Lincoln and midnineteenth-century America.

Originally published in August 2003
Reprint R0308D

The New World Disorder

NICOLAS CHECA, JOHN MAGUIRE, AND
JONATHAN BARNEY

Executive Summary

ON JANUARY 1, 1995, representatives from 76 countries signed the World Trade Organization charter, which for years had been part of a temporary trade agreement. The WTO's emergence as a fully empowered supranational body seemed to reflect the triumph of what the first President Bush had described as the "new world order."

That order was based on two assumptions: that a healthy economy and a sound financial system make for political stability, and that countries in business together do not fight each other. The number one priority of U.S. foreign policy was thus to encourage the former Communist countries of Europe and the developing nations in Latin America, Asia, and Africa to adopt business-friendly policies. Private capital would flow from the developed world into these countries, creating economic growth.

It sounded too good to be true, and so it proved. The world order of Bush *père* and his successor, Bill Clinton, has been replaced by the new world disorder of Bush *fils*. Under the second Bush's administration, the economic and political rationale behind the Washington consensus of the 1990s has unraveled, forcing a radical change in our perceptions of which countries are safe for business. Negotiating this new environment will require companies to more rigorously evaluate political events and more carefully assess the links between political, economic, and financial risk factors. They'll need to be more selective about which markets to enter, and they'll need to think differently about how to position themselves in those markets.

The geopolitical events of the past year, the Bush administration's global war on terror, as well as ongoing convulsions in traditional political and economic relationships must be understood and managed by corporate leaders worldwide. With careful analysis, business leaders can increase their companies' visibility and better respond to the uncertainties of the new world disorder.

ON JANUARY 1, 1995, at a very public ceremony in Geneva, representatives from 76 countries affixed their signatures to the charter of the World Trade Organization. The moment had been more than half a century in the making; the WTO was the last of the children of Bretton Woods to come of age. Its sister bodies—including the International Monetary Fund and the World Bank—were all formed in the 1940s. But the WTO had for years been classified as part of a temporary trade agreement. Its final emergence as a fully empowered supranational body seemed to reflect the triumph of what the first President Bush had described as the "new world order." That order was largely based on two assumptions: first, that a healthy economy and sound financial system make for political stability, and second, that countries in business together do not fight each other. U.S. foreign policy's number one priority was clear: to encourage the former Communist countries of Europe and the developing nations in Latin America, Asia, and Africa to adopt business-friendly policies. Private capital would then flow from the developed world into these countries, creating economic growth and jobs. When free enterprise took hold, so the argument went, traditional grievances, resentments, and hostilities would fade. As people liked to say, no two countries with McDonald's had ever gone to war with each other.

The policy was backed with lots of money, in the form of direct aid, loans from multilateral lending institutions such as the IMF, and a liquid market for governments to issue bonds to international private-sector investors. Perhaps the most dramatic instance of this support was the U.S.-led bailout of Mexico after the so-called Tequila Crisis of 1994. In effect, the United States and other developed countries were sending a message: Adopt economic reform, and we will be there to bail you out if your economy gets into trouble.

This reform path, often called the Washington Consensus, involved fiscal discipline, trade liberalization, privatization, deregulation, and expanded property rights through legal reforms. Promoters of these reforms hoped the changes would make developing countries more attractive to foreign investment and would integrate those countries even further into a competitive, but peaceful, global economic network. In its most extreme form, the vision became one in which these countries would become part of a liberal, open world economy that promoted Western values such as democracy. For most of the 1990s, the developing countries were more than happy to oblige. By August 2000, with the membership of Albania, the number of WTO members had nearly doubled to 139. In the early 1990s, Latin American governments ushered in a raft of currency reforms, from Argentina's currency board (1991) to Brazil's Real Plan (1994). Eastern European countries, meanwhile, launched bold crash courses in privatization, including the Czech voucher program (1992) and Russia's preelection privatizations (1996), as well as more gradual efforts by Hungary, Poland, and other countries. Aggressive modernization and reform in Southeast Asia earned the region's countries the sobriquet "tiger economies."

The U.S. policy of putting business first made the world a much simpler place for managers. Many assumed that the export of capital from developed economies to less-developed markets could be sustained indefinitely; as soon as a country chose to be integrated into the new global economy, its institutions would adapt under the same relentless pressure that was transforming enterprises around the world. Corporations could afford, therefore, to downplay political concerns in making decisions about investing in overseas markets.

For corporations it essentially boiled down to size: The bigger the country, the better and the safer. It seemed more dangerous to stay out of the large developing economies than to plunge in. A billion Chinese would buy an awful lot of cars, toothpaste, or shoes—and the early birds would catch the most worms. Financial investors had a similarly carefree attitude. As long as a country's currency could be freely exchanged and a liquid market was available in its debt, that country's economy was considered safe. When the IMF was behaving as lender of last, and in some cases first, resort (even though it never claimed to be), what did it matter if a country's banking system was compromised?

It sounded too good to be true, and so it proved. The new world order of Bush *père* and his successor, Bill Clinton, has been replaced by the new world disorder of Bush *fils*. Under the second Bush's administration, the economic and political rationale behind the Washington Consensus of the 1990s has unraveled, forcing a radical change to our perceptions of which countries are and are not safe for business. Negotiating this new environment will require companies to more rigorously evaluate political events and their contexts than they are used to doing and more carefully assess the links between the political, economic, and financial factors of risk. The new world disorder raises the potential risks and rewards of the specific tactical choices companies make. They will need to be more careful in selecting which markets to enter and how to position themselves in them. (The exhibit "Risk in the New World Disorder" summarizes how the risk factors have changed.)

From Order to Disorder

It was in the late 1990s that we got our first taste of financial globalization's downside: Thailand's 1997 financial crisis set off another in Korea the same year. The economic virus spread to Russia the following year, and in early 1999, Brazil was forced to abandon its fixed exchange rate policy. These countries had little in common, yet the financial crises propagated from one to the next like a virus because of the links created by the new global economy.

The reason was simple: Although the destinations of foreign direct investment were far flung and diverse, the source of that capital was not. The Western bank that held Thai baht also held Brazilian real. The fund that owned Korean bonds also held Russian bills. In the belief that the IMF, with the United States behind it, was willing to bail out economies that ran into short-term trouble, many of these institutions had loaded up on these assets. Once a crisis started, however, these institutions had to reassess the risk of their entire emerging market portfolios. Such a reassessment would precipitate a progressive sell-off, with assets in the weaker countries going first.

Risk in the New World Disorder

With the change in U.S. international global policy, nearly all the basic assumptions about political, economic, and financial risks have been turned on their heads. The following table summarizes the changes.

Risks	New World Order	New World Disorder
Political	More economic reform is better. Is the government pro-reform?	Future reform is less likely. How strong are local institutions?
Economic	Continued world growth and convergence are inevitable. The business cycle is finished. How big is the market?	Growth is less certain and the business cycle more volatile. Convergence is less likely. Where is the market?
Financial	The United States can't afford to let big markets fail. How liquid are the capital markets?	The United States will bail out only its strategic allies. How important is the country to the Pentagon?

At first, the IMF stepped in to help, but the costs of repeated multilateral bailouts became less and less affordable. Eventually, the Russian government defaulted, rendering near worthless the almost $40 billion in domestic government debt held by financial institutions and more than halving the $100 billion value of Russian equities. The United States did use its leverage to compel the IMF to aid Russia just prior to August 1998; however, it managed to buy less than a month of additional solvency. With the benefit of hindsight, we can see that investors' belief that the United States would stand behind large, reform-willing countries had triggered a speculative bubble in those economies that was to burst with the Russian default.

But not only the commitment and ability of the developed world to supply economic support was called into question. The developing countries were also proving less than successful at introducing the structural reforms that were supposed to be their side of the bargain. The forces of globalization had changed Russia's institutions so little that one civil servant characterized public-sector aid to Russia as "water poured onto a sheet of glass." Privatization programs were shown to have done little more than enrich the ruling classes, even as ordinary people paid for the supposed economic liberalization with their jobs. The hostility that this engendered among the often newly enfranchised voters only deepened as foreign investors began turning off the taps.

Ironically, the second President Bush put the final nail in the coffin of the new world order. Even before September 11, the administration was signaling that it had a very different vision of international engagement from its predecessor's, one based on security, not economic concerns. And security was now defined not just in the narrow Cold War terms of safety from attack from a hostile, though stable, superpower, but very broadly to include safety from terrorism and weapons of mass destruction, as well as vital economic inputs such as oil.

In May 2001, President Bush and Vice President Cheney's national energy policy stated, "Energy security must be a priority of U.S. trade and foreign policy. We must look beyond our borders and restore America's credibility with overseas suppliers. In addition, we must build strong relationships with energy-producing nations in our own hemisphere, improving the outlook for trade, investment, and reliable supplies."

The implication was clear: Security, in this case energy security, was now the foremost consideration in U.S. trade and foreign policy. The *National Security Strategy of the United States of America* published in September 2002 shows how the thinking developed from there. It has become very clear that the Bush government defines international engagement in terms of bilateral relationships with strategically important allies and unilateral confrontation with almost everybody else.

With the United States less willing to provide the developing world with economic support, the incentive for those governments to support pro-business reforms has diminished. After initially backing more economic integration with the United States, the Mexican government under Vicente Fox has turned decidedly populist. Among other things, that means less progress on trade issues, such as the Mexican desire to renegotiate some aspects of the North American Free Trade Agreement. No longer can it be assumed that the Mexican government (or the U.S. government, for that matter) is working to advance long-term convergence (in such matters as wages, interest rates, and inflation) between the two economies. The night that Vicente Fox won the 2000 election, an event that at last brought full democracy to Mexico, may ultimately prove to have been a high-water mark for Mexican economic reform.

Bush's new foreign policy chiefly means that the U.S. government will base its decisions on whether or not it will provide economic support less on a country's economic policies and market size and more on its importance to U.S. national and international security. From a business perspective, such an approach means companies should no longer assume the developed world's macroeconomic policy will consist of marginal monetary adjustments and gradual fiscal consolidation. This completely changes the calculus of market entry, exit, and risk management decisions. Developing countries once considered a sure bet for business have become a lot less safe. Others, meanwhile, despite patchy economic performance, are looking stronger.

Argentina has been one of the biggest victims of the United States' new policy focus. In the 1990s, it had a succession of pro-reform governments, each of which hewed so close to the Washington Consensus that Argentina was often referred to as the "IMF's star pupil." Argentina's international credit remained strong—even as it piled up a mountain of external debt—partly out of investors' belief that the IMF could not let the exemplar of its policy prescription fail. Today, Argentina is far from being America's darling. Not only has the country defaulted to private creditors, but it has even failed to make payments on debts to the World Bank. One IMF official described the fund's most recent agreement with Argentina as "the divorce agreement."

The performance of markets in countries of great strategic importance to the developed world, by contrast, has been remarkable. Turkey is the most obvious example. Back in the 1990s, Turkey found that its fractured political system was preventing it from making adequate fiscal and banking reforms. Those issues continue to worsen, yet even in the face of an unpredictable election, Turkish assets rose during the second half of 2002. Why? Financial markets judged that the United States would not let a Muslim ally suffer financial collapse.

Indeed, it is now widely recognized that Turkey has to jump through fewer hoops to obtain IMF and U.S. aid than it used to. The new priority being placed on Turkey's geographic position and its role-model status as a secularized Muslim state means that it has privileged access. Of course, Turkey's strategic importance is an old story. In the new world disorder, however, the value to the United States of Turkey's stability and geographic location is far more palpable and immediate than it was before. (Another region that looks promising is the Indian subcontinent. See "Opportunities in the New World Disorder" at the end of this article.)

Even developed economies are affected, albeit in a more nuanced way, by the sea change in the geopolitical outlook. The acrimony raised in the debate over Iraq is unlikely to result in a trade war, but it will have a small but perceptible effect on the way the United States and European Union address certain issues. These include trade disputes, U.S. legislative extraterritoriality, and competition regulations.

Once again, the estrangement between the United States and its European allies has been several years in the making, for the new administration came into office determined not to let existing alliances constrain America's freedom of action. Indeed, last September's national security strategy document makes only passing references to NATO and Western Europe. Thus, the consequences of this "assertiveness" will probably linger well after Congress starts eating French fries again.

Contextualizing Political Events

In coming to grips with the new world disorder, a business leader must first develop a detailed sense of the geopolitical outlook for the company's future strategic horizon. Essentially, the challenge is to develop a detailed scenario for the period under consideration. Without the discipline of a road map, managers typically react to events as they happen, ignoring their broader context and, therefore, completely misreading their significance. All too often this results in a highly volatile and short-term approach to investing in developing countries.

Past investment in Russia provides a perfect case study of this dynamic. Investors made the mistake of interpreting the victory of Boris Yeltsin over the Communist Party candidate in 1996 as a sign that Russia was safe for business. Since the Communists were bad, Yeltsin must be good, right? Plus, the United States had a clear interest in the stability (at almost any cost) of the nation because Russia was then the world's largest nuclear arsenal. To be sure, the Russian legal system's capricious nature deterred a lot of business investment and kept many a Western company from hurting itself. Nevertheless, plenty of Westerners and Western capital flowed in, making Moscow one of the most expensive cities in the world.

After the 1997 default, devaluation, and debt moratorium, Russia went from being perceived as the world's brightest investment opportunity to being the worst. The new perception took such firm hold that investors almost completely missed the Russian recovery of 1999 to 2000. At that time, higher oil prices, the appointment of Vladimir Putin as prime minister in August 1999, his assumption of the presidency in January 2000, and his subsequent election to the post in August 2000 combined to transform Russia's economic and political landscape. Rating agencies noticed the improvement only toward the end of 2000; Standard & Poor's, for example, raised Russian long-term external debt from SD (default) to C only as late as December 2000. And the equity market didn't take note of Russia's much-improved position until 2001.

Today, the temptation is to assume that the September 11 terrorist attacks led to a reversal of the U.S. attitude toward Russia and, along with it, a sharp reduction in the risk of doing business there. Wrong again—on both sides of the hypothesis. The United States viewed Russia as a strategic partner *before* the attacks.

In May 2001, the administration released a comprehensive energy policy that implied that the United States was seeking to diversify its energy imports to reduce reliance on unstable regimes in the Middle East. Russia was clearly one of the intended beneficiaries of the new U.S. policy. The September 11 attack and the subsequent war with Iraq will actually make Russia strategically less important to the United States. With the removal of Afghanistan's Taliban and Iraq's Saddam Hussein, the U.S. government is betting that the Middle East will become more stable, especially if Iraqi reconstruction goes well. This will reduce the U.S. need for Russian oil.

In the immediate aftermath of September 11, the Russian government firmly aligned itself with the United

States. But that alignment was the result of Putin's hasty assessment of Russia's economic interests and diplomatic influence, especially in the sensitive Commonwealth of Independent States, near Afghanistan. A few visits to Russia's Central Asian neighbors showed the Russian president that his country did not have enough influence to prevent a sizable American presence from developing as the war against the Taliban drew near. At the same time, Kremlin personnel convinced Putin of the economic value of a better relationship with the United States.

Historians will come to recognize that the alignment was purely temporary. By the end of 2002, the Russians had become well aware that their leverage over the United States would decline once hostilities in Iraq commenced, which was precisely why they were so opposed to the war during the UN negotiations early this year. What's more, the government had little to lose, but plenty to gain, from disapproval of the United States. Russian parliamentary elections are to occur in December; the presidential election will take place next year—and defying the Americans plays well to the domestic gallery.

In the long run, Russian and American disengagement from each other may have more serious repercussions in terms of Russia's domestic stability. Kremlin nervousness over the outcome of the elections—despite the lack of a viable alternative to Putin—has already prompted the government to roll back some of the liberalizing reforms of the post-Soviet era. Increased state control of the media, a key aim of the Putin Kremlin, is now complemented by a reconstitution of the old KGB under a new name. Long gone are the heady Yeltsin days when the West in general and the United States in particular were seen as the source of economic success and political truth.

If we had just one recommendation for managers to make, it would be to read the September 2002 *National Security Strategy*. (See "Shifting Strategies Revealed" at the end of this article.) The document provides great insight into the current Bush administration's thinking, but it hasn't proved to be a perfect policy guide, as the United States' evenhanded treatment of India and Pakistan reveals.

The Links Between Risks

All managers recognize in theory that they have to look at the three factors (political, economic, and financial) of country risk together to get a sense of the totality of risks and opportunities. The trouble is, systematic analyses typically end up crudely aggregating the three factors, which is often why managers fail to predict sudden and dramatic crises that with hindsight they recognize as having been inevitable. Corporate leaders are not alone; international financial institutions such as the IMF, World Bank, and Inter-American Development Bank are struggling with the same issues.

Instead of merely cataloging the different risks, managers and policy makers need to look more closely at the links between them. When risks are linked, then a local problem can easily escalate into an international crisis.

Let's take a closer look at Argentina, which exemplifies this dynamic. On the face of it, the country was a low-risk prospect. To be sure, it had a high amount of external debt, but the country's banking system was the strongest in Latin America, in large measure because its currency, the peso, was freely convertible, placing a premium on sound monetary policy. As a result, Argentina had no trouble accessing international capital markets. The economic story also looked reassuring. Argentina had miraculously tamed the hyperinflation of the early 1990s. The recession of the late 1990s—caused by the financial dislocation of the Asian crisis—could seemingly be reversed by a rather straightforward, if unpleasant, fiscal adjustment. The new de la Rua government had pledged to do that. The party alliance that brought Fernando de la Rua to office was fragile, but Argentina's strong presidential system had allowed Carlos Menem to put through far more difficult policies than anything de la Rua would have to enact.

Or so it would appear. Unfortunately, the underlying political fractures, in both de la Rua's Alianza party and the Peronist opposition fatally compromised all aspects of fiscal planning. Provincial governors had tremendous power over national politics as well as claims to the federal budget. Once the provincial governors decided to confront the weak Alianza government, the fiscal adjustment needed to close the public finance gap went from manageable to enormous. As soon as debt holders caught wind of the problem, Argentina's debt load went from "no problem" to "unsustainable" overnight. The Argentine government then forced the banks to buy government debt at rates they would not accept in a free market.

As the crisis continued to wear on, and Clinton's administration was replaced by Bush's administration, Washington dithered over the appropriate response, finally giving an aid package that did little to avoid what had become inevitable. Ultimately, Argentina defaulted, floated its currency, imposed capital controls, and nearly abandoned functional democratic processes. Anyone looking only at the economics of Argentina on the eve of the debt crisis would have seen a country actually beginning to emerge from a bad recession. A strictly financial analysis would not have identified Argentina as a leading candidate for crisis, the country having survived the crises that forced the Russian government to default on its domestic government bonds and Brazil to devalue its currency. Politically, Argentina had been able to prosper throughout the 1990s under the same party system and federal structure that prevailed on the threshold of the crisis. Argentina's institutions seemed sound. But the favorable outlook for each of the risk factors was vulnerable to latent weaknesses in the other factors. The economic recovery relied on Argentina's ability to continue to borrow on international capital markets. That ability in turn depended upon not just strong political institutions but also on effective political will to maintain necessary fiscal discipline. With the government's fiscal discipline in question, markets demanded higher yields to take on the higher risk of Argentine debt. That damaged the economic recovery, further weakening the government and setting up the vicious cycle whose end point we all know.

Ironically, companies that rely heavily on local experts are often the most likely to miss the signals for the kind of sudden crisis that arose in Argentina. The sheer volume and specificity of local experts' knowledge inevitably create a compelling picture of the political and economic environment in which a company operates. But specificity of knowledge does not preclude error: All the local experts in Argentina in 2001 "knew" that

Finance Minister Domingo Cavallo would fix the economy or "knew" that the IMF would always bail out Argentina. Local experts may provide useful eyes and ears on the ground but are not in a position to know how U.S. or NGO policies will affect the country where they are based. These policies, made by outsiders, will frequently affect the local environment far more than will events on the ground. Local experts, in our experience, invariably are oblivious to the significance of broader international events. Overreliance on local information sources eventually leads senior managers to confuse descriptive detail with accuracy and completeness of analysis.

Tactics Are Critical

When it comes to investing in today's unstable environment, companies' tactical choices about market entry and management matter a great deal more than they did in the 1990s. They mattered less then because the operating environment was more predictable. For instance, a company operating in Argentina at that time did not really have to worry about the mechanics of incorporation, financing, and ownership—above and beyond the usual issues of tax treatment and other efficiencies—of, say, a fully owned subsidiary in Buenos Aires. Under the 1:1 convertibility peg, the transfer of dollars or pesos from the subsidiary to the parent or vice versa was a normal event, similar to such actions between, for instance, U.S. and UK branches of an international corporation.

But the changing political environment is turning traditional market entry logic on its head. Foreign direct investment in Russia is a case in point. Under Yeltsin's unstable regime, the threat of a Communist resurgence in 1996, and the sheer chaos of switching to a market economy, joint ventures had long seemed a much safer way to enter the Russian market than plunging into the deep end with large-scale foreign direct investment. Yet recently, BP purchased the Russian energy company TNK from its two Russian owners, Alfa Bank and Renova. Why did BP choose this route?

First, the change in U.S. energy policy created new incentives to participate in the Russian energy industry. Second, despite the pretense of reform, in many ways Russia has taken backward steps on some issues dear to foreign investors. In the energy sector in particular, the Production Sharing Agreement has been effectively gutted. This law was formed in 1999 to encourage foreign investment in Russian energy development by sheltering foreign companies in some joint ventures from onerous (and arbitrary) Russian taxes. More generally, minority shareholder rights are as tenuous as ever. This partial repudiation of international standards by the Russian government has made investment in that country today an all-or-nothing game.

The changing political climate is also overturning conventional marketing wisdom. For instance, many pundits argue that the current consumer backlash against U.S. products in the Middle East is here to stay and may spread to other countries. For instance, Coca-Cola—perhaps the most potent commercial symbol of America—has a new competitor in the Middle East. That competitor is Mecca-Cola, which is produced by a Tunisian-born French entrepreneur and is targeting Muslim consumers. Mecca-Cola's value proposition is to mimic Coca-Cola's branding (complete with the red and white label) but to promise 20% of its profits to Palestinian and Muslim charities. Mecca-Cola is rapidly establishing its brand as the anti–Coca-Cola through such publicity efforts as its sponsorship of an antiwar demonstration held in London last February. Currently, it claims to have received orders for 16 million bottles, including a million each in France and the United Kingdom.

Mecca-Cola is not the only entrant trying to target the world's billion-plus Muslim cola consumers and tap into the prevailing anti-American sentiment. Other entrants include Zam Zam Cola, an Iranian product that was developed after Pepsi was banned from the country in 1979, and British-based Qibla Cola (slogan: "Liberate your taste"), a name that refers to the direction Muslims face when praying to Mecca. These products have just launched in Europe as well.

On the face of it, companies like Coca-Cola ought to respond to this backlash by building or acquiring a local rather than an American image through joint ventures, the purchase of local brand names, and so forth. Yet once again, conventional wisdom can be deceptive.

Raytheon, one of the world's leading defense companies, has chosen to trumpet its American identity rather than downplay it. Raytheon believes that success on the military front is good news for the company and its products—since the United States is a winner, then Raytheon, as a natural extension of U.S. security, will be a winner, too. This tactic turns the potential liability of being part of the hated empire into an asset. Of course, it would be difficult for a company like Raytheon to de-Americanize its brand. But joining the winning team is certainly a viable tactic for any firm whose customer base includes national governments. It may also prove to be a better long-term approach for consumer products, which could explain why companies like Coca-Cola have adopted a wait-and-see attitude.

WHATEVER THE FUTURE HOLDS, one thing is certain: Interdependence between countries will only increase. The crises in Asia, Latin America, and Russia illustrated how closely linked economies are across the globe, as well as how quickly international finance can change, long before the world had to confront a new global political and security reality. The geopolitical events of the past year, the Bush administration's global war on terror, as well as ongoing convulsions in traditional political and economic relationships, have now added another layer of complexity that must be understood and managed by corporate and financial leaders worldwide. Yet as we have shown, with careful analysis business leaders can increase their companies' visibility and better respond to the uncertainties of the new world disorder.

Opportunities in the New World Disorder

BUSINESSES CAN'T PLAY DEFENSE all the time; only offense puts points on the board. Since globalization is here to stay, transnational corporations need to take risks—or risk being left behind.

In our view, Pakistan and India represent one of the biggest opportunities in the new world disorder. For different reasons, both countries have long been underperformers. Pakistan has been seen as almost a failed state, one prone to political instability, with an unreliable security service that is uncomfortably close to radical Islamic groups. India, despite its educated workforce, has languished under a bloated bureaucracy and entrenched domestic interests. In addition, both nuclear powers are locked in a poisonous, chronic conflict over Kashmir. On the face of it, this does not appear to be a promising region for investment.

It is also tempting to think that the new confrontational approach of the United States toward Islamic terrorism would add fuel to a very dangerous fire on the subcontinent. The Bush administration's "war on terror" would seem to be a clear negative for the region. What's more, the administration's rhetoric would also seem to imply that only one country stands to gain from the new geopolitical reality.

Since India and Pakistan were always at each other's throats over Kashmir, surely the Bush "with us or against us" philosophy meant that the United States would have to favor one country over the other. The *National Security Strategy of the United States of America* published in September 2002 specifically mentions India as a partner, along with China and Russia, in forging a "new consensus on basic principles" for a system of security alliances.

But these impressions are turning out to be false. First of all, Pakistan has been a prime beneficiary of the U.S. policy shift, winning massive debt forgiveness. Meanwhile, the problems posed by both sides' possession of nuclear weapons have forced U.S. engagement whenever the regional dispute begins to seriously escalate. The nature of the India–Pakistan conflict—a Cold War in miniature—makes country risk almost perfectly symmetric: A diplomatic failure in Pakistan will also be a diplomatic failure in India, and vice versa. Pakistan got the most obvious short-term bribe, but India will gain, too. In fact, the Indian subcontinent provides a textbook example of how the United States has had to adapt its stated policies to complex regional politics.

To be sure, it is impossible to predict the future, and foolhardy to claim that the Kashmir conflict is forever contained. Pakistan is still a mess socially, politically, and economically. India is still a country of great potential, but one with a long way to go. But the new priority on security means that the subcontinent's overall level of risk, though still high, is falling. The region deserves a second look.

Shifting Strategies Revealed

ALTHOUGH PRESS COVERAGE of the September 2002 edition of the *National Security Strategy of the United States of America* has focused primarily on the concept of preemption (the United States specifically authorizing military action before it or its interests are attacked), the document marks perhaps the most significant shift in U.S. strategy since World War II. It foreshadowed, for instance, some of the difficulties in NATO during the run-up to the war with Iraq.

For a start, the document makes only one mention of Europe and NATO: Europe is exhorted to increase its economic growth, and NATO is asked to change to accommodate the new challenges and threats it faces. Indeed, the document seems to imply that NATO will be superseded by a new system of regional alliances, which will be anchored by Russia, China, and India. It suggests that such a system cannot function as NATO did during the Cold War. That's even assuming the intended partners' foreign policy goals are well aligned with those of the United States, which they are not. The only criterion linking these countries as anchors of an "alternative to great power competition" is the common interest in fighting the global terrorist threat and the proliferation of weapons of mass destruction. Implied in the document is that these three countries are the geographic front line for containing a fundamentalist Muslim threat emanating from the Middle East.

Even if it's not the ultimate in policy guides, the document is a revealing lens through which to view the current Bush administration's mind-set.

Originally Published in August 2003
Reprint R0308E

In Search of Global Leaders

STEPHEN GREEN, FRED HASSAN,
JEFFREY IMMELT, MICHAEL MARKS, AND
DANIEL MEILAND

Executive Summary

FOR ALL THE TALK ABOUT global organizations and executives, there's no definitive answer to the question of what we really mean by "global." A presence in multiple countries? Cultural adaptability? A multilingual top team? We asked four CEOs and the head of an international recruiting agency—HSBC's Stephen Green, Schering-Plough's Fred Hassan, GE's Jeffrey Immelt, Flextronics's Michael Marks, and Egon Zehnder's Daniel Meiland—to tell us what they think.

They share some common ground. They all agree, for example, that the shift from a local to a global market-place is irreversible and gaining momentum. "We're losing sight of the reality of globalization. But we should pay more attention, because national barriers are quickly coming down," Daniel Meiland says. "If you look ahead five or ten years, the people with the top jobs in large corporations . . . will be those who have lived in several cultures and who can converse in at least two languages."

But the CEOs also disagree on many issues—on the importance of overseas assignments, for instance, and on the degree to which you need to adhere to local cultural norms. Some believe strongly that the global leader should, as a prerequisite to the job, live and work in other countries. As Stephen Green put it, "If you look at the executives currently running [HSBC's] largest businesses, all of them have worked in more than one, and nearly all in more than two, major country markets." Others downplay the importance of overseas assignments. "Putting people in foreign settings doesn't automatically imbue new attitudes, and it is attitudes rather than experiences that make a culture global," says Fred Hassan.

The executives' essays capture views that are as diverse and multidimensional as the companies they lead.

FOR ALL THE TALK ABOUT global organizations and executives, there's no definitive answer to the question of what, exactly, we mean by "global." A presence in multiple countries? Cultural adaptability? A multilingual executive team? We asked four CEOs and the head of an international recruiting agency—all leaders of companies that would by any definition be characterized as global—to contribute their thoughts.

They found some common ground. All agreed, for example, that the shift from a local to a global marketplace is irreversible and gaining momentum. And most felt that personal attention from senior management was a critical factor in developing global capabilities. But they differed in other respects—on issues such as the importance of overseas assignments and the degree to which businesspeople need to adhere to local cultural norms. Their essays, which follow, capture a range of ideas that are as diverse and multidimensional as the companies they run.

Stephen Green
Group CEO, HSBC

When I joined HSBC in 1982, it was essentially an Asian company, although it did own 51% of Marine Midland Bank in New York. We had around 30,000 employees at that time, mostly English and Cantonese speakers. Today's HSBC is a very different organization, employing some 215,000 people across the globe. Of the United Nations' six official languages, our employees are very well represented in all but one.

We expanded mostly by means of acquisition, starting with the Midland Bank in the UK—a deal that doubled the size of HSBC, gave us a European presence, and broadened our range of services. Later, we also bought CCF in France. Outside Europe, our acquisitions included Bamerindus in Brazil, Grupo Financiero Bital in Mexico, and, this year, Household Finance in the United States. Today, our assets are evenly distributed between Europe, Asia, and the Americas. We are unusual among the world's largest banks in that significantly less than half our profits come from any one jurisdiction. Even the largest banks typically have three-quarters or more of their profits coming from one home base. In 2002, no single jurisdiction accounted for more than 40% of our profits.

Despite the enormous changes in its demographics and business, HSBC has retained a remarkably consistent corporate identity. That's largely because of the way we develop our senior management team. No one gets to the top at HSBC without having worked in more than one market. If you look at the executives currently running the company's largest businesses, all of them have worked in more than one, and nearly all in more than two, major country markets. We strongly believe, as many others do, that travel broadens the mind. And if travel alone does that, just think how much more you get from living and working in different countries.

Most of our recruits are recent university graduates. We tend not to go out of our way to look for MBAs or people in their thirties. In fact, I think it's a mistake for companies to have too much of their top talent join their organizations in mid-career. (Though I should admit that I was a mid-career recruit myself!) Our recruitment process is sophisticated, involving a complex process of tests, interviews, and exercises. We don't look so much at what or where people have studied but rather at their drive, initiative, cultural sensitivity, and readiness to see the world as their oyster. Whether they've studied classics, economics, history, or languages is irrelevant. What matter are the skills and qualities necessary to be good, well-rounded executives in a highly international institution operating in a diverse set of communities.

In fact, HSBC has long been famous for its cadre of global executives, formerly known as international officers. We now call them international managers, which sounds less militaristic. They are hired with the expectation that they will spend their entire careers with the institution and also be very mobile. But we don't limit our international development to these managers. HSBC will give any promising executive who expresses an interest in gaining international exposure the opportunity to work overseas. Take the chief operating officer of our UK business. He's a Welshman in his early fifties. Until about five years ago, he had never worked outside the United Kingdom—for his entire career, he had been a UK-based executive at the former Midland Bank. One day, he put his hand up and said, "I'm willing to go overseas," and so we made him country manager for India. He spent three years there and took to it like a duck to water, later becoming country manager for Malaysia, one of our biggest Southeast Asian businesses, before taking up his current job.

Twenty years ago, most of our top recruits came from British schools and universities, and today's top team reflects that bias. But we now have many able non-British managers in our ranks due to recent acquisitions. Today, we recruit at 68 universities worldwide, this year hiring people from 38 different countries, so that our team of the future will be much more representative of our geographic spread of businesses.

Because of our recruitment and development practices, many of our people have worked in multiple countries—some emerging, some developed—and in different sorts of businesses, from retail and wholesale to banking and insurance. These global employees act as a kind of organizational glue for the company.

The fact that they have all had those experiences also means that many of them have a great deal in common. A British manager with international experience will tend to identify more with a Japanese manager with international experience than he will with another manager who has worked in only her home country. But that doesn't mean that we're trying to develop identikit

managers. Far from it. If, for example, my French colleagues lost their Frenchness or my Brazilian colleagues
lost their Brazilian-ness, life would be a lot duller, and
HSBC would be a lot less profitable. We prize our diversity. That's all part of the richness and fun of working
together, and it's what makes us so creative and responsive to our clients' needs.

Fred Hassan
Chairman and CEO, Schering-Plough

In the 1960s and 1970s, conventional wisdom held that
the way to create a global culture was to move employees
around and place them in multiple cultures. But that system often didn't work very well; putting people in foreign
settings doesn't automatically imbue new attitudes, and
it is attitudes rather than experiences that make a culture global. Recruiting people with the "right" education
or with foreign language skills doesn't guarantee that
people have the right attitude either. I've met many people who speak three or four languages yet still have a very
narrow view of the world. At the same time, I've come
across people who speak only English but have a real
passion and curiosity about the world and who are very
effective in different cultures.

Having a global attitude is not the same as being able
to imitate local styles. It's just as important for managers
to be themselves. I spent 17 years working for a Swiss
company as a U.S. resident. In the 1970s, it was considered forward in Switzerland to address people by their
first names. But while I would address my superiors
using their last names, with my peers and subordinates I

followed the U.S. standard of using first names. People were okay with this because they knew I was not being false. Being yourself while also showing interest and openness is at the heart of a global attitude.

In the research-based pharmaceuticals industry, employees must have global attitudes if their companies are to survive. And in my new role leading Schering-Plough, I will focus on building those attitudes. Our industry is product driven. We have long lead times—it can take five to 15 years for a new product to be born. Individual product bets are into hundreds of millions, if not billions, of dollars. Once you've got an idea that's been turned into a product, you need to pay back the high cost of R&D, so you need to sell it around the world. Good ideas can come from anywhere, and good products can be sold anywhere. The more places you are, the more ideas you will get. And the more ideas you get, the more places you can sell them and the more competitive you will be. Managing in many places requires a willingness to accept good ideas no matter where they come from—which means having a global attitude.

Creating a global attitude was at the heart of the turnaround I led as CEO of Pharmacia & Upjohn. When I joined the company in 1997, it had just gone through the very difficult merger of the U.S.-based Upjohn and the Sweden-based Pharmacia. It was difficult largely because of the serious disconnect between the two corporate cultures—not at all unusual when you bring together two large companies, especially if they're based in different countries. The cultural differences seriously undermined the newly merged company's ability to exploit its winning products. Our research labs in Kalamazoo, for example, had developed an excellent new antibiotic called Zyvox. But the drug was being ignored by many country managers in Europe because they lacked confidence in Kalamazoo's ability to do research. We went through a big change process at Pharmacia & Upjohn to end that kind of thinking. We established new performance expectations that measured how well our employees demonstrated open-minded behaviors, including shared accountability, transparency, and collaboration across geographies. We called this behavior-based management and made it central to performance evaluation.

I invited executives to reflect on these new expectations and to decide whether they were on board. In the end, 12 of the top 20 executives were moved out of their positions. The others stayed on, and the team became very productive because its members all shared a strong commitment to behavior-based management. After the changes, Zyvox was approved and was rolled out in just 12 months in all three major drug markets. In the past at that company, you would have seen very little interest abroad, and even introducing it in one market would have taken years.

My experience with that change process convinced me that identifying and developing people with global attitudes requires personal involvement from the top. The CEO has to see himself as the chief developer of talent, no matter how large the company. In 2000, we merged Pharmacia & Upjohn with Monsanto to create Pharmacia Corporation, a company with about 43,000 employees worldwide. I made it my business to know that large organization's top 200 managers personally—I don't mean the top 200 according to hierarchy, but according to their potential and the degree to which they contributed to the company's goals. Some of these people were quite junior, but I tried to know who they were, what their strengths and weaknesses were, and I looked at their performance evaluations. In my last six months there, I had one-on-one meetings with approximately half of these people.

I also like to be on the front lines to observe how people are working. When I go to a sales meeting, I don't sit with the brass from headquarters; I sit with sales reps. In 2000, I went to the American Society of Clinical Oncology meeting, the biggest oncology convention in the world. Typically only sales and marketing people attend; I was the only "big pharma" CEO there. All of this contact is time-consuming, but it allows me to keep my ear to the ground, to overcome any hierarchical barriers.

Avon's Andrea Jung takes the same kind of personal approach to identifying and nurturing global talent. She keeps a close eye on high-potential managers even though they may be two or three or four levels below her, and she goes over the list at a private dinner once a year with the board. Her management team is graded not only on how it selects new managers but also on what it does to develop them as contributors to the global community. She's created a very powerful, very effective business culture in a truly global company, which has much of its sales outside North America. In the past, Avon was very decentralized and had many different cultures in different countries. But Andrea was able to strike a balance such that country managers are now very strong and very well plugged in to the local environment but also responsible for passing on best practices to their colleagues in other locations.

That's the essence of a global culture. The country is still important, and the local country manager is in charge and accountable, but he or she is part of a global network and feels a sense of belonging. I once met with some of Pharmacia's local sales reps in a remote town in China. I mentioned that we were rolling out a new stock option program to our sales representatives around the world, and I saw their eyes immediately light up. It wasn't the money or the stock that mattered to them as much as the knowledge that they were receiving some of the same incentives as our U.S. reps.

Jeffrey Immelt
Chairman and CEO, General Electric

A good global company does three things. It's a global sales company—meaning it's number one with customers all over the world, whether in Chicago or Paris or Tokyo. It's a global products company, with technologies, factories, and products made for the world, not just for a single region. And most important, it's a global people company—a company that keeps getting better by capturing global markets and brains.

How do you make all these things happen?

First, human resources has to be more than a department. GE recognized early on—50 or 60 years ago—that in a multi-business company, the common denominators are people and culture. From an employee's first day at GE, she discovers that she's in the people-development business as much as anything else. You'll find that most good companies have the same basic HR processes that we have, but they're discrete. HR at GE is not an agenda item; it is the agenda.

We run the company so that 300,000 people feel the chairman might enter their world at any time. I spend roughly 40% of my time on people issues; so do our other top leaders. I teach at the Learning Center in Crotonville three or four times a month. In the course of a year, I will review, in detail, five or six thousand internal résumés through a process we call Session C. During that session, I'm not locked in a room with executives; I'll see 300 people. And I like to spend time in the field with sales reps who've been identified as having high potential. A swing through Europe is filled with employee meetings—some hard-nosed business reviews, some big customer meetings with sales reps, and some meetings with factory teams. I try to reach down into the organization very hard, all the time. When I meet people who especially impress me, right away I call our HR director Bill Conaty and say, "I want these three people to get a double dip of stock options." The recognition and reinforcement are immediate. As soon as someone rewards them for their talents, these star performers begin to aim even higher.

Second, we devote a lot of time and energy to building up personal networks. This is a big company in a big world. You can't be a lone ranger and also be a global manager. We spend $1 billion on training, which has the most important benefit of connecting people across the company. We also move people around a lot, for the same reason. When I meet someone, I don't quiz him to see if he can do the job; I expect that. I don't look for smoothness. I don't look for "GE-isms." I look for a person with a great instinctive feel for his market, his business, and his subordinates. I always ask people about their teams. I want people who bring other people with them. When I do a Session C, half the grade I give is to the individuals and half is to their team. I ask, "Who's in your wallet?" I want to see who's in their family, who they brought with them in their career. Some people's wallets have no pictures. Some can pull out a whole family album. That is extremely important.

Third, the culture needs to be performance oriented. Without a meritocracy, you get cronyism and homogeneity rather than a culture open and broad enough to get the best from everybody. We're still too homogeneous, but we've made a lot of progress. When I first joined General Electric, globalization meant training the Americans to be global thinkers. So Americans got the expat assignments. We still have many Americans living around the world and that's good, but we shifted our emphasis in the late 1990s to getting overseas assignments for non-Americans. Now you see non-Americans doing new jobs, big jobs, important jobs at every level and in every country.

A lot of people have said that GE could be more global by moving its headquarters overseas—for example, by moving its medical systems business from Milwaukee to Paris. That's a relic of the strategy of making Americans more global. It's more important to find the best people, wherever they may be, and develop them so that they can lead big businesses, wherever those may be. It's truly about people, not about where the buildings are. You've got to develop people so they are prepared for leadership jobs and then promote them. That's the most effective way to become more global.

The ultimate evidence that a business has become a global people company is the talent it attracts; it matters to us that we get the best talent. We try very hard to provide a company, a set of values, and a culture that employees can be proud of, whether it be in Pittsfield, Paris, Shanghai, or London. We still don't get all the talent we want. In Germany, for instance, we sometimes lose the best talent to Siemens. I go to Germany every time I'm in Europe. I give talks at universities and try to convince people that GE is a better company with more career opportunities. Twenty years ago in Japan, we found it almost impossible to hire people. If a top student told his parents he was going to work for GE, they would just about disown him.

That's changed. The business community has gone global, and it can't go back. Career decisions are no longer based on nationalism. The last time I was in Europe, I visited Insead. These young people want to work for GE—or Citigroup or Goldman Sachs; they don't say, "It's only Siemens for me." I can now recruit great people in Japan. Lee Scott, the CEO of Wal-Mart, tells me his big challenge today is globalization. If he wants to keep growing at the rate he desires, he has to go to Europe, China, and so on. And that's Wal-Mart, good old American Wal-Mart.

Michael Marks

CEO, Flextronics

About ten years ago, right after NAFTA took effect, I had the idea of locating a Flextronics manufacturing plant in Mexico. I clearly remember people saying to me, "Don't do it. That's a siesta culture," implying that any labor or other cost savings to be gained there would be offset by the workers' laziness. I made a trip anyway and checked out three factories, one making cables for the auto industry, one making toasters, and one doing electronic assembly. I came away thinking, "It's not humanly possible to work harder than these people or to produce products faster than this." We built a plant near Guadalajara in 1997, and within five years, its revenues grew to more than $1 billion.

I tell the story because it underscores the corrosive effect of stereotypes and how they undermine good decision making in a business that needs to globalize. To me, the most important criterion for a business leader is that he or she be free of such strong biases. If I heard evidence of that kind of stereotyping in conversations with a job candidate, that would be a big red flag.

Usually, of course, the stereotyping is more subtle. Managers often pick up the impression that the Chinese are good at this, the Germans are good at that, and so on. But I have learned that in every place we operate, in every country, the people want to do a good job. They simply need training. If you show people, for instance, what great manufacturing is, they will work toward it— and I have found that there is no place where people can't do a world-class job.

This isn't to say that we approach every region with a cookie-cutter uniformity. We may need to train workers differently in different parts of the world. We discovered this early on in Guadalajara because the demographics of Mexico are very young—a large percentage of the workforce is under the age of 35. The contrast with Japan, a company with a relatively old workforce, is striking. Training becomes a different proposition when you cannot rely on tacit knowledge transfer from seasoned 50 year olds to greener 30 year olds. Mexico might require a more intense training regimen or a longer time commitment.

Running a global company also means learning how different countries are governed and being able to work with their leaders. This is particularly true for a manufacturer like Flextronics, because most countries, whether developing or developed, tend to want the manufacturing jobs we have to offer. As a consequence, we must be in frequent contact with senior government officials, addressing issues like tax holidays and dollars for training. Consider an issue that the head of our European operation is currently dealing with. A few years back, the Hungarian government agreed to give us a ten-year tax holiday as the result of a $50 million capital investment there. The problem is, Hungary is now trying to gain admittance to the European Union, which won't allow such tax holidays. What will we do about this? It will get worked out, but it's complicated. The head of European operations has to have the skills to deal with such high-level political issues—skills that don't develop in people automatically.

How do we choose leaders with the cultural breadth to conduct such negotiations—and to get past the kind of stereotypes I discussed earlier? The most capable executives I've known have traveled extensively, learned other languages, and have often been educated abroad. But most of them gained their broad perspectives in the course of their work. Flextronics' top management team orchestrates manufacturing activity in 28 different countries and leads sales operations worldwide. The peer group includes a CFO from New Zealand, a CTO from Grenada, a sales executive from Ireland, and business unit heads from Sweden, Great Britain, India, Singapore, and Hong Kong. It's hard to work in such an environment and remain provincial in your outlook.

Increasingly, though, we are seeing that our more junior executives have this kind of multicultural exposure as part of their upbringing. Today's 30 year olds grew up in a different world from their parents', with much greater ease of travel, more education abroad, and technologies like the Internet and cell phones affording more lines of global communication. Dream résumés that show, say, an upbringing in Paris, a Harvard MBA, and summer internships in Japan are becoming more and more common among young job applicants. As a result, there is much more uniformity among young managers around the world. Imagine pulling together 30 people from 30 different countries, all in their thirties. Chances are, they would all interact quite easily—and that isn't because young people tend to be fairly open-minded. It's because there's been a major shift in thinking from the last generation. And that shift will make the task of developing global leaders easier with each passing year. In another two decades, an American is not going to stop to consider that he is dealing with someone from Japan. A strong leader will be just that—a strong leader—whether Brazilian or Malaysian. The global part of leadership will be a given.

Daniel Meiland

Executive Chairman, Egon Zehnder International

The world is getting smaller, and markets are getting bigger. In my more than 25 years in the executive search profession, we've always talked about the global executive, but the need to find managers who can be effective in many different settings is growing ever more urgent. In addition to looking for intelligence, specific skills, and technical insights, companies are also looking for executives who are comfortable on the world stage.

And yet we have a lot to learn. Over the years, about half of our big searches have been for people with truly international experience, but in only a small fraction of those cases did we end up hiring foreigners to the country where an organization was based. Many companies haven't been all that successful at developing global executives from within either. The intentions are good, but the fact is, practice hasn't caught up with intent. One problem is that many companies still believe the best way to help managers develop a global mind-set is to put them in positions in other countries. But that hasn't been very effective, primarily because companies station people abroad and then forget about them. If anything, advancement is even more difficult for the expat when he returns to headquarters, having missed out on opportunities to network with top management. Also, many people have reasons for not wanting to hop from location to location. For one, it's easier to develop client relationships if you stay in one place for an extended period of time. Those client relationships can be very important when it comes to getting promoted.

The companies that do handle these rotations well—Shell and General Electric come to mind—track their people carefully over the course of many years. GE has systems for examining people's work histories and designing their next steps toward becoming global leaders. And Shell has done a particularly good job of giving people not only major responsibilities abroad but also great opportunities for advancement when they return. Another example is McKinsey consulting, which in 1994 elected Rajat Gupta as the first non-American to run the firm. Gupta is a truly global executive and has shown a great deal of cultural sensitivity.

Cultural sensitivity doesn't always come naturally, so developing global executives often requires helping people to see their own biases. Many years ago, when I first started at Egon Zehnder International, I was working on an assignment in the greater China area, and I criticized a team member directly for the way he handled a project. I was told later that in China it's not good to criticize someone face-to-face; it ends up being counterproductive, and there are other ways to get the message across. This is fairly common knowledge today, but back then it was not. The feedback I got was critical to developing my own cultural sensitivity.

But while you need to be aware and accepting of cultural norms, you also need to remember that people are pretty much the same everywhere. The respect you must show for different cultures isn't all that different from the respect you must show to people in your own culture. The executive who truly respects his employees and peers as human beings will always win. Find reasons to praise performance and to show a real interest in your employees—not just when and where it matters to you personally, say, at headquarters, but with everyone, at every level. And you should always be genuine.

Developing a global mind-set and learning about other cultures are important for your career, of course, but they're also enriching on a very personal level. We all need to experience other cultures and ideas to grow as individuals. And to some degree, that individual growth intertwines with the professional. An American, the new CEO of Zurich Financial brought with him a true and very personal love of various cultures. And he came from a very different industry—consulting and auditing. Put together, his diverse personal and professional experiences have given him unique and insightful perspectives on the company's challenges.

We're living in a special time, with our minds on war and terrorism, and we're losing sight of the reality of globalization. But we should pay attention, because national barriers are quickly coming down. If you look ahead five to ten years, the people with the top jobs in large corporations, even in the United States, will be those who have lived in several cultures and who can converse in at least two languages. Most CEOs will have had true global exposure, and their companies will be all the stronger for it.

Originally published in August 2003
Reprint R0308B

What Is a Global Manager?

CHRISTOPHER A. BARTLETT AND
SUMANTRA GHOSHAL

Executive Summary

RIVEN BY IDEOLOGY, RELIGION, and mistrust, the world seems more fragmented than at any time since, arguably, World War II. But however deep the political divisions, business operations continue to span the globe, and executives still have to figure out how to run them efficiently and well. In "What Is a Global Manager?" (first published in September–October 1992), business professors Christopher Bartlett and Sumantra Ghosal lay out a model for a management structure that balances the local, regional, and global demands placed on companies operating across the world's many borders.

In the volatile world of transnational corporations, there is no such thing as a "universal" global manager, the authors say. Rather, there are three groups of specialists: business managers, country managers, and functional managers. And there are the top executives at a corporate headquarters who manage the complex interactions between the three—and can identify and develop the talented executives a successful transnational requires. This kind of organizational structure characterizes a transnational rather than an old-line multinational, international, or global company. Transnationals integrate assets, resources, and diverse people in operating units around the world. Through a flexible management process, in which business, country, and functional managers form a triad of different perspectives that balance one another, transnational companies can build three strategic capabilities: global-scale efficiency and competitiveness; national-level responsiveness and flexibility; and cross-market capacity to leverage learning on a worldwide basis.

Through a close look at the successful career of Leif Johansson of Electrolux, Howard Gottlieb of NEC, and Wahib Zaki of Procter & Gamble, the authors illustrate the skills that each managerial specialist requires.

I N THE EARLY STAGES of its drive overseas, Corning Glass hired an American ex-ambassador to head up its international division. He had excellent contacts in the governments of many nations and could converse in several languages, but he was less familiar with Corning and its businesses. In contrast, ITT decided to set up a massive educational program to "globalize" all managers responsible for its worldwide telecom business—in essence, to replace the company's national specialists with global generalists.

Corning and ITT eventually realized they had taken wrong turns. Like many other companies organizing for worldwide operations in recent years, they found that an elite of jet-setters was often difficult to integrate into the corporate mainstream; nor did they need an international team of big-picture overseers to the exclusion of focused experts.

Success in today's international climate—a far cry from only a decade ago—demands highly specialized yet closely linked groups of global business managers, country or regional managers, and worldwide functional managers. This kind of organization characterizes a *transnational* rather than an old-line multinational, international, or global company. Transnationals integrate assets, resources, and diverse people in operating units around the world. Through a flexible management process, in which business, country, and functional managers form a triad of different perspectives that balance one another, transnational companies can build three strategic capabilities: global-scale efficiency and competitiveness; national-level responsiveness and flexibility; and cross-market capacity to leverage learning on a worldwide basis.

While traditional organizations, structured along product or geographic lines, can hone one or another of these capabilities, they cannot cope with the challenge of all three at once. But an emerging group of transnational companies has begun to transform the classic hierarchy of headquarters-subsidiary relationships into an integrated network of specialized yet interdependent units. For many, the greatest constraint in creating such an organization is a severe shortage of executives with the skills, knowledge, and sophistication to operate in a more tightly linked and less classically hierarchical network.

In fact, in the volatile world of transnational corporations, there is no such thing as a universal global manager. Rather, there are three groups of specialists: business managers, country managers, and functional managers. And there are the top executives at corporate headquarters, the leaders who manage the complex interactions between the three—and can identify and develop the talented executives a successful transnational requires.

To build such talent, top management must understand the strategic importance of each specialist. The careers of Leif Johansson of Electrolux, Howard Gottlieb of NEC, and Wahib Zaki of Procter & Gamble vividly exemplify the specialized yet interdependent roles the three types of global managers play.

The Business Manager
Strategist + Architect + Coordinator

Global business or product-division managers have one overriding responsibility: to further the company's global-scale efficiency and competitiveness. This task requires not only the perspective to recognize opportunities and risks across national and functional boundaries but also the skill to coordinate activities and link capabilities across those barriers. The global business manager's overall goal is to capture the full benefit of integrated worldwide operations.

To be effective, the three roles at the core of a business manager's job are to serve as the strategist for his or her organization, the architect of its worldwide asset and resource configuration, and the coordinator of transactions across national borders. Leif Johansson, now president of Electrolux, the Sweden-based company, played all three roles successfully in his earlier position as head of the company's household appliance division.

In 1983, when 32-year-old Johansson assumed responsibility for the division, he took over a business that had been built up through more than 100 acquisitions over the previous eight years. By the late 1980s, Electrolux's portfolio included more than 20 brands sold in some 40 countries, with acquisitions continuing throughout the decade. Zanussi, for example, the big Italian manufacturer acquired by Electrolux in 1984, had built a strong market presence based on its reputation for innovation in household and commercial appliances. In addition, Arthur Martin in France and Zoppas in Norway had strong local brand positions but limited innovative capability.

As a result of these acquisitions, Electrolux had accumulated a patchwork quilt of companies, each with a different product portfolio, market position, and competitive situation. Johansson soon recognized the need for an overall strategy to coordinate and integrate his dispersed operations.

Talks with national marketing managers quickly convinced him that dropping local brands and standardizing around a few high-volume regional and global products would be unwise. He agreed with the local managers that their national brands were vital to maintaining consumer loyalty, distribution leverage, and competitive flexibility in markets that they saw fragmenting into more and more segments. But Johansson also understood the views of his division staff members, who pointed to the many similarities in product characteristics and consumer needs in the various markets. The division staff was certain Electrolux could use this advantage to cut across markets and increase competitiveness.

Johansson led a strategy review with a task force of product-division staff and national marketing managers.

While the task force confirmed the marketing managers' notion of growing segmentation, its broader perspective enabled Johansson to see a convergence of segments across national markets. Their closer analysis also refined management's understanding of local market needs, concluding that consumers perceived "localness" mainly in terms of how a product was sold (distribution through local channels, promotion in local media, use of local brand names) instead of how it was designed or what features it offered.

From this analysis, Johansson fashioned a product-market strategy that identified two full-line regional brands to be promoted and supported in all European markets. He positioned the Electrolux brand to respond to the cross-market segment for high prestige (customers characterized as conservatives), while the Zanussi brand would fill the segment where innovative products were key (for trendsetters).

The local brands were clustered in the other two market segments pinpointed in the analysis: yuppies ("young and aggressive" urban professionals) and environmentalists ("warm and friendly" people interested in basic-value products). The new strategy provided Electrolux with localized brands that responded to the needs of these consumer groups. At the same time, the company captured the efficiencies possible by standardizing the basic chassis and components of these local-brand products, turning them out in high volume in specialized regional plants.

So, by tracking product and market trends across borders, Leif Johansson captured valuable global-scale efficiencies while reaping the benefits of a flexible response to national market fragmentation. What's more, though he took on the leadership role as a strategist, Johansson never assumed he alone had the understanding or the ability to form a global appliance strategy; he relied heavily on both corporate and local managers. Indeed, Johansson continued to solicit guidance on strategy through a council of country managers called the 1992 Group and through product councils made up of functional managers.

In fact, the global business manager's responsibility for the distribution of crucial assets and resources is closely tied to shaping an integrated strategy. While he or she often relies on the input of regional and functional heads, the business manager is still the architect who usually initiates and leads the debate on where major plants, technical centers, and sales offices should be located—and which facilities should be closed.

The obvious political delicacy of these debates is not the only factor that makes simple economic analysis inadequate. Within every operating unit there exists a pool of skills and capabilities that may have taken a lot of time and investment to build up. The global business manager has to achieve the most efficient distribution of assets and resources while protecting and leveraging the competence at hand. Electrolux's household appliance division had more than 200 plants and a bewildering array of technical centers and development groups in many countries. It was clear to Johansson that he had to rationalize this infrastructure.

He began by setting a policy for the household appliance division that would avoid concentration of facilities in one country or region, even in its Scandinavian home base. At the same time, Johansson wanted to specialize the division's development and manufacturing infrastructure on a "one product, one facility" basis. He was determined to allocate important development and manufacturing tasks to each of the company's major markets. In trying to optimize robustness and flexibility in the long term rather than minimize short-term costs, Johansson recognized that a specialized yet dispersed system would be less vulnerable to exchange-rate fluctuations and political uncertainties. This setup also tapped local managerial and technical resources, thereby reducing dependence on the small pool of skilled labor and management in Sweden.

Instead of closing old plants, Johansson insisted on upgrading and tailoring existing facilities whenever possible. In addition to averting political fallout and organizational trauma, Electrolux would then retain valuable know-how and bypass the start-up problems of building from scratch. An outstanding example of this approach is Zanussi's Porcia plant in Italy, which Electrolux turned into the world's largest washing machine plant. After a massive $150 million investment, the Porcia plant now produces 1.5 million units a year.

Although acquisition-fueled growth often leads to redundancy and overcapacity, it can also bring new resources and strengths. Instead of wiping out the division's diversity through homogenization or centralization, Johansson decided to leverage it by matching each unit's responsibilities with its particular competence. Because of the Scandinavian flair for modular design, he assigned the integrated kitchen-system business to Electrolux's Swedish and Finnish units. He acknowledged Porcia's experience in component production by consolidating design and production of compressors there. Johansson's reshaping of assets and resources not only enhanced scale economies and operational flexibility but also boosted morale by giving operating units the opportunity to leverage their distinctive competences beyond their local markets.

Newly developed business strategies obviously need coordination. In practice, the specialization of assets and resources swells the flow of products and components among national units, requiring a firm hand to synchronize and control that flow. For organizations whose operations have become more dispersed and specialized at the same time that their strategies have become more connected and integrated, coordination across borders is a tough challenge. Business managers must fashion, a repertoire of approaches and tools, from centralized control to management of exceptions identified through formal policies to indirect management via informal communication.

Leif Johansson coordinated product flow—across his 35 national sales units and 29 regional sourcing facilities—by establishing broad sourcing policies and transfer-pricing ranges that set limits but left negotiations to internal suppliers and customers. For instance, each sales unit could negotiate a transfer price with its internal source for a certain product in a set range that was usually valid for a year. If the negotiations moved outside that range, the companies had to check with headquarters. As a coordinator, Johansson led the deliberations that defined the logic and philosophy of the parameters; but he stepped back and let individual unit managers run their own organizations, except when a matter went beyond policy limits.

In contrast, coordination of business strategy in Johansson's division was managed through teams that cut across the formal hierarchy. Instead of centralizing, he relied on managers to share the responsibility for monitoring implementation and resolving problems through teams. To protect the image and positioning of his regional brands—Electrolux and Zanussi—he set up a brand-coordination group for each. Group members came from the sales companies in key countries, and the chairperson was a corporate marketing executive. Both groups were responsible for developing a coherent, pan-European strategy for the brand they represented.

To rationalize the various product strategies across Europe, Johansson created product-line boards to oversee these strategies and to exploit any synergies. Each product line had its own board made up of the corporate product-line manager, who was chair, and his or her product managers. The Quattro 500 refrigerator-freezer, which was designed in Italy, built in Finland, and marketed in Sweden, was one example of how these boards could successfully integrate product strategy.

In addition, the 1992 Group periodically reviewed the division's overall results, kept an eye on its manufacturing and marketing infrastructure, and supervised major development programs and investment projects. Capturing the symbolic value of 1992 in its name, the group was chaired by Johansson himself and included business managers from Italy, the United Kingdom, Spain, the United States, France, Switzerland, and Sweden.

Indeed, coordination probably takes up more of the global business manager's time than any other aspect of the job. This role requires that a manager have great administrative and interpersonal skills to ensure that coordination and integration don't deteriorate into heavy-handed control.

Many traditional multinational companies have made the mistake of automatically anointing their home country product-division managers with the title of global business manager. Sophisticated transnational companies, however, have long since separated the notions of coordination and centralization, looking for business leadership from their best units, wherever they may be. For example, Asea Brown Boveri (ABB), the Swiss-headquartered electrical engineering corporation, has tried to leverage the strengths of its operating companies and exploit their location in critical markets by putting its business managers wherever strategic and organizational dimensions coincide. In ABB's power-transmission business, the manager for switch gear is located in Sweden, the manager for power transformers is in Germany, the manager for distribution transformers is in Norway, and the manager for electric metering is in the United States.

Even well-established multinationals with a tradition of tight central control are changing their tack. The head of IBM's telecommunications business recently moved her division headquarters to London, not only to situate the command center closer to the booming European market for computer networking but also "to give us a different perspective on all our markets."

The Country Manager
Sensor + Builder + Contributor

The building blocks for most worldwide companies are their national subsidiaries. If the global business manager's primary objective is to achieve global-scale efficiency and competitiveness, the national subsidiary manager's is to be sensitive and responsive to the local market. Country managers play the pivotal role not only in meeting local customer needs but also in satisfying the host government's requirements and defending their company's market positions against local and external competitors.

The need for local flexibility often puts the country manager in conflict with the global business manager. But in a successful transnational like Electrolux, negotiation can resolve these differences. In this era of intense competition around the world, companies cannot afford to permit a subsidiary manager to defend parochial interests as "king of the country."

Nor should headquarters allow national subsidiaries to become the battleground for corporate holy wars fought in the name of globalization. In many companies, the national subsidiaries are hothouses of entrepreneurship and innovation—homes for valuable resources and capabilities that must be nurtured, not constrained or cut off. The subsidiaries of Philips, for one, have consistently led product development: In television, the company's first color TV was developed in Canada, the first stereo model in Australia, and the first teletext in the United Kingdom.

Unilever's national subsidiaries have also been innovative in product-marketing strategy: Germany created the campaign for Snuggle (a fabric softener); Finland developed Timotei (an herbal shampoo); and South Africa launched Impulse (a body perfume).

In fact, effective country managers play three vital roles: the sensor and interpreter of local opportunities and threats, the builder of local resources and capabilities, and the contributor to and active participant in global strategy. Howard Gottlieb's experience as general manager of NEC's switching-systems subsidiary in the United States illustrates the importance of all three of these tasks.

As a sensor, the country manager must be good at gathering and sifting information, interpreting the implications, and predicting a range of feasible outcomes. More important, this manager has the difficult task of conveying the importance of such intelligence to people higher up, especially those whose perceptions may be dimmed by distance or even ethnocentric bias. Today, when information gathered locally increasingly applies to other regions or even globally, communicating effectively is crucial. Consumer trends in one country often spread to another; technologies developed in a leading-edge environment can have global significance; a competitor's local market testing may signal a wider strategy; and national legislative initiatives in areas like deregulation and environmental protection tend to spill across borders.

Gottlieb's contribution to NEC's understanding of changes in the telecommunications market demonstrates how a good sensor can connect local intelligence with global strategy. In the late 1980s, Gottlieb was assigned to build the U.S. market for NEAX 61, a widely acclaimed digital telecom switch that was designed by the parent company in Japan. Although it was technologically sophisticated, early sales didn't meet expectations.

His local-market background and contacts led Gottlieb to a quick diagnosis of the problem. NEC had designed the switch to meet the needs of NTT, the Japanese telephone monopoly, and it lacked many features that customers in the United States wanted. For one thing, its software didn't incorporate the protocol conversions necessary for distributing revenues among the many U.S. companies that might handle a single long-distance phone call. Nor could the switch handle revenue-enhancing features like call waiting and call forwarding, which were vital high-margin items in the competitive, deregulated American market.

In translating the needs of his U.S. division to the parent company, Gottlieb had a formidable task. To convince his superiors in Japan that redesigning NEAX 61 was necessary, he had to bridge two cultures and penetrate the subtleties of the parent company's Japanese-dominated management processes. He had to instill a sense of urgency in several corporate management groups, varying his pitches to appeal to the interests of each. For instance, Gottlieb convinced the engineering department that the NEAX 61 switch had been underdesigned for the U.S. market and the marketing department that time was short because the Bell operating companies were calling for quotes.

A transnational's greater access to the scarcest of all corporate resources, human capability, is a definite advantage when compared with strictly local companies—or old-line multinationals, for that matter. Scores of companies like IBM, Merck, and Procter & Gamble have recognized the value of harvesting advanced (and often less expensive) scientific expertise by upgrading local development labs into global centers of technical excellence.

Other companies have built up and leveraged their overseas human resources in different ways. Cummins Engine, for example, has set up its highly skilled but surprisingly low-cost Indian engineering group as a worldwide drafting resource; American Airlines's Barbados operation handles much of the corporate clerical work; and Becton Dickinson, a large hospital supply company, has given its Belgian subsidiary pan-European responsibility for managing distribution and logistics.

Indeed, the burden of identifying, developing, and leveraging such national resources and capabilities falls on country managers. Howard Gottlieb, after convincing Tokyo that the United States would be an important market for NEC's global digital-switch design, persuaded headquarters to permit his new engineering group to take part early on in the product development of the next-generation switch—the NEAX 61E. He sent teams of engineers to Japan to work with the original designers; and, to verify his engineers' judgments, Gottlieb invited the designers to visit his customers in the United States. These exchanges not only raised the sensitivity of NEC's Japan-based engineers to U.S. market needs but also significantly increased their respect for their American colleagues. Equally important, the U.S. unit's morale rose.

As a builder, Gottlieb used this mutual confidence as the foundation for creating a software-development capability that would become a big corporate asset. Skilled software engineers, very scarce in Japan, were widely available in the United States. Gottlieb's first move was to put together a small software team to support local projects. Though its resources were limited, the group turned out a number of innovations, including a remote software-patching capability that later became part of the 61E switch design. The credibility he won at headquarters allowed Gottlieb to expand his design engineering group from ten to more than 50 people within two years, supporting developments not only in North America but also eventually in Asia.

In many transnationals, access to strategically important information—and control over strategically important assets—has catapulted country managers into a much more central role. As links to local markets, they are no longer mere implementers of programs and policies shaped at headquarters; many have gained some influence over the way their organizations make important strategic and operational decisions. In most of today's truly transnational companies, country managers and their chief local subordinates often participate in product-development committees, product-marketing task forces, and global-strategy conferences. Even at the once impenetrable annual top management meetings, national subsidiary managers may present their views and defend their interests before senior corporate and domestic executives—a scenario that would have been unthinkable even a decade ago.

Of course, the historic position of most national units of worldwide companies has been that of the implementer of strategy from headquarters. Because the parent company's accepted objectives are the outcome of discussions and negotiations involving numerous units, divisions, and national subsidiaries, sometimes a country manager must carry out a strategy that directly conflicts with what he or she has lobbied for in vain.

But a diverse and dispersed worldwide organization, with subsidiaries that control many of the vital development, production, and marketing resources, can no longer allow the time-honored "king of the country" to decide how, when, and even whether his or her national unit will implement a particular strategic initiative. The decision made by the North American subsidiary of Philips to outsource its VCRs from a Japanese competitor rather than the parent company is one of the most notorious instances of how a local "king" can undermine global strategy.

At NEC, Howard Gottlieb spent about 60% of his time on customer relations and probing the market and about 30% managing the Tokyo interface. Gottlieb's ability to understand and interpret the global strategic implications of U.S. market needs—and the software-development group he built from scratch—let him take part in NEC's ongoing strategy debate. As a result, he changed his division's role from implementer of corporate strategy to active contributor in designing that strategy.

The Functional Manager
Scanner + Cross-Pollinator + Champion

While global business managers and country managers have come into their own, functional specialists have yet to gain the recognition due them in many traditional multinational companies. Relegated to support-staff roles, excluded from important meetings, and even dismissed as unnecessary overhead, functional managers are often given little chance to participate in, let alone contribute to, the corporate mainstream's global activity. In some cases, top management has allowed staff functions to become a warehouse for corporate misfits or a graveyard for managerial has-beens. Yet at a time when information, knowledge, and expertise have become more specialized, an organization can gain huge benefits by linking its technical, manufacturing, marketing, human resources, and financial experts worldwide.

Given that today's transnationals face the strategic challenge of resolving the conflicts implicit in achieving global competitiveness, national responsiveness, and worldwide learning, business and country managers must take primary responsibility for the first two capabilities. But the third is the functional manager's province.

Building an organization that can use learning to create and spread innovations requires the skill to transfer specialized knowledge while also connecting scarce resources and capabilities across national borders.

To achieve this important objective, functional managers must scan for specialized information worldwide, "cross-pollinate" leading-edge knowledge and best practice, and champion innovations that may offer transnational opportunities and applications.

Most innovation starts, of course, when managers perceive a particular opportunity or market threat, such as an emerging consumer trend, a revolutionary technological development, a bold competitive move, or a pending government regulation. When any of these flags pops up around the world, it may seem unimportant to corporate headquarters if viewed in isolation. But when a functional manager serves as a scanner, with the perspective and expertise to detect trends and move knowledge across boundaries, he or she can transform piecemeal information into strategic intelligence.

In sophisticated transnationals, senior functional executives serve as linchpins, connecting their areas of specialization throughout the organization. Using informal networks, they create channels for communicating specialized information and repositories for proprietary knowledge. Through such links, Electrolux marketing managers first identified the emergence of cross-market segments and NEC's technical managers were alerted to the shift from analog to digital switching technology.

In the same manner, Wahib Zaki of Procter & Gamble's European operations disapproved of P&G's high-walled organizational structures, which isolated and insulated the technical development carried out in each subsidiary's lab. When Zaki became head of R&D in Europe, he decided to break down some walls. In his new job, he was ideally placed to become a scanner and cross-pollinator. He formed European technical teams and ran a series of conferences in which like-minded experts from various countries could exchange information and build informal communication networks.

Still, Zaki needed more ammunition to combat the isolation, defensiveness, and "not invented here" attitude in each research center. He distributed staff among the European technical center in Brussels and the development groups of P&G's subsidiaries. He used his staff teams to help clarify the particular role of each national technical manager and to specialize activities that had been duplicated on a country-by-country basis with little transfer of accumulated knowledge.

In response to competitive threats from rivals Unilever, Henkel, and Colgate-Palmolive—and to a perceived consumer trend—P&G's European headquarters asked the Brussels-based research center to develop a new liquid laundry detergent. By that time, Zaki had on hand a technical team that had built up relationships among its members so that it formed a close-knit network of intelligence and product expertise.

The team drew the product profile necessary for healthy sales in multiple markets with diverse needs. In several European markets, powdered detergents contained enzymes to break down protein-based stains, and the new liquid detergent would have to accomplish the same thing. In some markets, a bleach substitute was important; in others, hard water presented the toughest challenge; while in several countries, environmental concerns limited the use of phosphates. Moreover, the new detergent had to be effective in large-capacity, top-loading machines, as well as in the small front-loading machines common in Europe. Zaki's team developed a method that made enzymes stable in liquid form (a new technique that was later patented), a bleach substitute effective at low temperatures, a fatty acid that yielded good water-softening performance without phosphates, and a suds suppressant that worked in front-loading machines (so bubbles wouldn't ooze out the door). By integrating resources and expertise, Zaki cross-pollinated best practice for a new product.

The R&D group was so successful that the European headquarters adopted the use of teams for its management of the new brand launch. P&G's first European brand team pooled the knowledge and expertise of brand managers from seven subsidiaries to draft a launch program and marketing strategy for the new liquid detergent Vizir, which ensured its triumphant rollout in seven countries in six months. P&G's homework enabled it to come up with a product that responded to European needs, while Colgate-Palmolive was forced to withdraw its liquid detergent brand, Axion—which had been designed in the United States and wasn't tailored for Europe—after an 18-month market test.

As a reward for his performance in Europe, Wahib Zaki was transferred to Procter & Gamble's Cincinnati corporate headquarters as a senior vice president of R&D. He found that researchers there were working on improved builders (the ingredients that break down dirt) for a new liquid laundry detergent to be launched in the

United States. In addition, the international technology-coordination group was working with P&G's Japanese subsidiary to formulate a liquid detergent surfactant (the ingredient that removes greasy stains) that would be effective in the cold-water washes common in Japanese households, where laundry is often done in used bathwater. Neither group had shared its findings or new ideas with the other, and neither had incorporated the numerous breakthroughs represented by Vizir—despite the evidence that consumer needs, market trends, competitive challenges, and regulatory requirements were all spreading across national borders.

Playing the role of champion, Zaki decided to use this development process to demonstrate the benefits of coordinating P&G's sensitivity and responsiveness to diverse consumer needs around the world. He formed a team drawn from three technical groups (one in Brussels and two in the United States) to turn out a world liquid laundry detergent. The team analyzed the trends, generated product specifications, and brought together dispersed technical knowledge and expertise, which culminated in one of Procter & Gamble's most successful product launches ever. Sold as Liquid Tide in the United States, Liquid Cheer in Japan, and Liquid Ariel in Europe, the product was P&G's first rollout on such a global scale.

As Zaki continued to strengthen cross-border technology links through other projects, Procter & Gamble gradually converted its far-flung sensing and response resources into an integrated learning organization. By scanning for new developments, cross-pollinating best practice, and championing innovations with transnational applications, Wahib Zaki, a superlative functional manager, helped create an organization that could both develop demonstrably better new products and roll them out at a rapid pace around the world.

The Corporate Manager
Leader + Talent Scout + Developer

Clearly, there is no single model for the global manager. Neither the old-line international specialist nor the more recent global generalist can cope with the complexities of cross-border strategies. Indeed, the dynamism of today's marketplace calls for managers with diverse skills. Responsibility for worldwide operations belongs to senior business, country, and functional executives who focus on the intense interchanges and subtle negotiations required. In contrast, those in middle management and frontline jobs need well-defined responsibilities, a clear understanding of their organization's transnational mission, and a sense of accountability—but few of the distractions senior negotiators must shoulder.

Meanwhile, corporate managers integrate these many levels of responsibility, playing perhaps the most vital role in transnational management. The corporate manager not only leads in the broadest sense; he or she also identifies and develops talented business, country, and functional managers—and balances the negotiations among the three. It's up to corporate managers to promote strong managerial specialists like Johansson, Gottlieb, and Zaki, those individuals who can translate company strategy into effective operations around the world.

Successful corporate managers like Floris Maljers, cochairman of Unilever, have made the recruitment, training, and development of promising executives a top priority. By the 1980s, with Maljers as chairman, Unilever had a clear policy of rotating its managers through various jobs and moving them around the world, especially early in their careers. Unilever was one of the first transnationals to have a strong pool of specialized yet interdependent senior managers, drawn from throughout its diverse organization.

But while most companies require only a few truly transnational managers to implement cross-border strategies, the particular qualities necessary for such positions remain in short supply. According to Maljers, it is this limitation in human resources—not unreliable or inadequate sources of capital—that has become the biggest constraint in most globalization efforts.

Locating such individuals is difficult under any circumstances, but corporate managers greatly improve the odds when their search broadens from a focus on home country managers to incorporate the worldwide pool of executives in their organization. Because transnationals operate in many countries, they have access to a wide range of managerial talent. Yet such access—like information on local market trends or consumer needs that should cross organizational boundaries—is often an underexploited asset.

As a first step, senior executives can identify those in the organization with the potential for developing the skills and perspectives demanded of global managers. Such individuals must have a broad, nonparochial view of the company and its operations yet a deep understanding of their own business, country, or functional tasks. Obviously, even many otherwise talented managers in an organization aren't capable of such a combination of flexibility and commitment to specific interests, especially when it comes to cross-border coordination and integration. Top management may have to track the careers of promising executives over several years before deciding whether to give them senior responsibilities. At Unilever, for example, the company maintains four development lists that indicate both the level of each manager and his or her potential. The progress of managers on the "A1" list is tracked by Unilever's Special Committee, which includes the two chairmen.

Once corporate managers identify the talent, they have the duty to develop it. They must provide opportunities for achievement that allow business, country, and functional managers to handle negotiations in a worldwide context. A company's ability to identify individuals with potential, legitimize their diversity, and integrate them into the organization's corporate decisions is the single clearest indicator that the corporate leader is a true global manager—and that the company is a true transnational.

Originally published in September–October 1992
Reprint R0308F

Thriving Locally
in the Global Economy

ROSABETH MOSS KANTER

Executive Summary

MORE AND MORE SMALL and midsize companies are joining corporate giants in striving to exploit international growth markets. At the same time, civic leaders worry about their communities' economic future in light of the impact of global forces on the operation and survival of businesses. How can communities retain local vitality yet still link their businesses to the global economy?

Harvard professor Rosabeth Moss Kanter addresses that question in this classic HBR article, originally published in 1995. To avoid a clash between international economic interests and local political interests, globalizing businesses must learn how to be responsive to the communities in which they operate, Kanter says. And communities must determine how to create a civic culture that will attract and retain footloose companies.

115

The author surveyed five U.S. regions with direct connections to the global economy—Boston, Cleveland, Miami, Seattle, and the Spartanburg-Greenville region of South Carolina—to determine their business and civic leaders' strategies for improving their constituents' quality of life. She identified ways in which the global economy can work locally by capitalizing on the resources that distinguish one place from another.

Kanter argues that regions can invest in capabilities that connect their local populations to the global economy in one of three ways: as *thinkers, makers,* or *traders.* She points to the Spartanburg-Greenville region as a good example of a world-class maker, with its exceptional blue-collar workforce that has attracted more than 200 companies from 18 countries. The history of the economic development of this region is a lesson for those seeking to understand how to achieve world-class status and bring local residents into the world economy.

IN THE FUTURE, success will come to those companies, large and small, that can meet global standards and tap into global networks. And it will come to those cities, states, and regions that do the best job of linking the businesses that operate within them to the global economy.

Sweeping changes in the competitive landscape, including the presence of foreign competitors in domestic markets, are driving businesses to rethink their strategies and structures to reach beyond traditional boundaries. Increasing numbers of small and midsize companies are joining corporate giants in striving to exploit international growth markets or in trying to become world-class even if only to retain local customers.

At the same time, communities are under considerable pressure to understand what they need to do to enhance—and in some cases even preserve—their local vitality. Local residents and civic leaders are expressing concern about their communities' economic future, particularly in light of the impact of global forces on where businesses locate and how they operate. Some see a basic conflict between social and community interests that are largely domestic or even local, and business competitiveness issues that often are international in scope. If the class division of the industrial economy was between capital and labor, or between managers and workers, the class division of the emerging information economy could well be between cosmopolitans with global connections and locals who are stuck in one place.

To avoid a clash between global economic interests and local political interests, businesses must know how to be responsive to the needs of the communities in which they operate even as they globalize. And communities must determine how best to connect cosmopolitans and locals and how to create a civic culture that will attract and retain footloose companies. The greatest danger to the viability of communities is not globalization but a retreat into isolationism and protectionism. In the global economy, those people and organizations that are isolated and cut off are at a disadvantage. They are targets for nativists who feed on discontent by blaming outsiders, scapegoating foreigners, and urging that barriers be erected to stem the global tide. But if communities retreat into isolationism, they are unlikely to solve the very problems that led to their discontent in the first place. Ironically, the best way for communities to preserve their local control is to become more competitive globally.

This lesson began to come into sharp focus for me in 1990, when I started to explore emerging business alliances and partnerships around the world. My Harvard Business School research group and I examined more than 37 companies operating in more than 15 countries. I saw that those companies often were surpassing their peers by linking forces in international networks. But I also saw how controversial their actions were in their own countries and cities, and how irrevocably they were altering life back home. What I saw made me wonder how the rise of a global economy changes the meaning of community, which is largely rooted in place. And I started thinking about how global forces could be marshaled to support and develop communities rather than cause their demise.

Beginning in 1993, I undertook a civic-action research project in five regions of the United States that connect with the global economy in different ways: the areas of Boston, Cleveland, Miami, Seattle, and Spartanburg and Greenville in South Carolina. By looking at those cities and regions through the lens of business, I was able to view local economies not as abstractions or aggregate statistics but as living and working centers for organizations struggling every day to make and sell goods and services. I could listen to what real people had to say about how they were faring. I was able to sound out business and civic leaders about their strategies for improving their constituents' economy and quality of life in light of the global changes. And I identified some ways in which the global economy can work locally by capitalizing on the availability of those resources that distinguish one place from another.

The New Criteria for Success

In the industrial economy, place mattered to companies because it gave them control over the means of production—capital, labor, and materials—and access to transportation centers that minimized the cost of moving products from one location to another. In the global information economy, however, power comes not from location per se but rather from the ability to command one of the intangible assets that make customers loyal. These assets are concepts, competence, and connections. Today a place has value if it can provide companies with at least one of these resources.

Concepts are leading-edge ideas, designs, or formulations for products or services that create value for customers. *Competence* is the ability to translate ideas into applications for customers, to execute to the highest standards. *Connections* are alliances among businesses to leverage core capabilities, create more value for customers, or simply open doors and widen horizons. Unlike tangible assets, these intangible resources are portable and fluid, and they decline rapidly in value if not constantly updated. World-class companies keep their supplies of these assets current by being more entrepreneurial, more learning oriented, and more collaborative. They continually seek better concepts and invest in innovation. They search for ideas and experience and nurture their people's knowledge and skills. And they seek partnerships with others to extend their competencies and achieve common objectives.

Companies have several ways of deriving concepts, competence, and connections from the communities in which they are located. Regions can be superior development sites for concepts because innovators can flourish there, come into contact with new ways of thinking, and find support for turning their ideas into viable businesses. Regions also can distinguish themselves by enhancing production competence through maintaining consistently high quality standards and a highly trained workforce. And they can provide connections to global networks in which businesses find resources and partners to link them with other markets. Cities can thrive as international centers if the businesses and the people who work for them can learn more and develop better by being there rather than somewhere else. Places can—and do—establish linkages to world-class companies by investing and specializing in capabilities that connect their local populations to the global economy in one of three ways: as thinkers, makers, or traders.

Thinkers specialize in concepts. Such places are magnets for brainpower, which is channeled into knowledge industries. Their competitive edge comes from continual innovation, and they set world standards in the export of both knowledge and knowledge-based products. Thinkers count on their absolute dominance in technological creativity and intellectual superiority to ensure their position on the world stage. The Boston area, for example, specializes in concepts—in creating new ideas and technologies that command a premium in world markets.

Makers are especially competent in execution. They have superior production skills and an infrastructure that supports high-value, cost-effective production. As a result, maker places are magnets for world-class manufacturing. Spartanburg and Greenville are good examples of world-class makers: They have an exceptional blue-collar workforce that has attracted more than 200 companies from many countries.

Traders specialize in connections. They sit at the crossroads of cultures, managing the intersections. They help make deals or transport goods and services across borders of all types. Miami, with its Latin American and increasingly global connections, is a quintessential trader city. Organizations such as AT&T selected Miami for their Latin American headquarters because of the city's Pan-American characteristics. Miami bridges Latino and Anglo cultures in the same way that Hong Kong and Singapore traditionally have linked British and Chinese cultures.

Boston, Miami, and Spartanburg and Greenville are distinctive as models of emerging international cities because of their emphasis on one core capability. Each must develop a broader range of capabilities for its success to continue, but their stories offer lessons for businesses and cities everywhere about how to harness global forces for local advantage. For example, through a combination of local and foreign leadership and influence, the Spartanburg-Greenville area systematically upgraded its ability to meet the needs of world-class manufacturers. The history of the region's economic development is a lesson for business and community leaders seeking to understand what is required to achieve world-class status and bring local residents into the world economy.

An Unlikely Success Story

Spartanburg and Greenville, in the hill country of South Carolina, make an unlikely center for international industry. Yet these neighboring cities are the site of the highest diversified foreign investment per capita in the United States. Their success rests on the second intangible asset: competence. By achieving superiority in their ability to produce goods, these cities have derived benefits from the global economy as makers.

As in other U.S. cities, the center of activity has shifted from downtown to the shopping malls and industrial belts on the periphery. But what is found on the outskirts of Spartanburg and Greenville, and throughout the seven-county area called the Upstate, is unusual: a concentration of foreign manufacturing companies on I-85, the interstate highway that stretches from Atlanta, Georgia, to Charlotte, North Carolina. The local section of this highway is known as "the autobahn" because of the many German companies located there.

For decades, business leaders have worked with civic leaders to shape an economic development strategy that is almost a foreign policy. For the Spartanburg-Greenville region, foreign investment has been a positive force, bringing benefits to local businesses, workers, and the community beyond the infusion of capital and job creation. The presence of foreign companies has unleashed and renewed entrepreneurship and innovation, stimulated learning, heightened awareness of world standards, and connected local companies to global networks.

The cities of Spartanburg (population 46,000) and Greenville (population 58,000) and the seven surrounding counties contain almost a million people and share an airport. The region has a diversified economic base that includes textiles, high technology, metalworking, and automobiles. Unemployment stays well below the national average, and the I-85 business belt boasts the largest number of engineers per capita in the United States and the country's lowest work-stoppage rate. South Carolina's nationally recognized worker training program has upgraded the workforce and raised the average wage rate across the region. The Upstate is now home to more than 215 companies from 18 countries, 74 of which have their U.S. headquarters there. The largest manufacturing employer is Michelin North America, which is a subsidiary of France's Michelin Groupe. It has three facilities in the region, a total investment of $1.5 billion, more than 9,000 employees in the state, and comparatively high factory wage rates of $15 to $16 per hour. R&D for Michelin North America is also located in Greenville, and a test track and distribution center are situated nearby. In 1985, the company moved its headquarters to Greenville.

The area entered the international limelight in 1992, at the time BMW announced it would locate its first-ever manufacturing facility outside Germany in Spartanburg County. Newspapers and magazines took note of the "boom belt" in the Southeast along I-85. The BMW facility promised to provide 2,000 jobs directly and create perhaps 10,000 more at a time when the U.S. auto industry was only beginning to emerge from recession and U.S. cities were desperate for sources of new employment. Ecstatic locals donned T-shirts proclaiming the arrival of "Bubba Motor Works."

BMW's announcement made international headlines and created a local stir because BMW is a well-known upscale consumer product and a household name. But behind this highly visible investment stood several decades of investment by companies that were not household names but that had contributed to the worldwide reputation for competence in industrial skills that would attract BMW to the area.

The history of economic development in the Upstate represents one model for success in the global economy: a solid base of midsize entrepreneurial companies that innovate continually in basic manufacturing and employ a workforce whose skills are regularly upgraded against world standards. Four factors are critical for success:

- visionary leaders who have a clear economic development strategy and who work actively to recruit international companies;

- a hospitable business climate and a positive work ethic that attract innovative manufacturing companies seeking to make long-term investments;

- customized training and gradual upgrading of workers' skills; and

- collaboration within the business community and between business and government to improve quality and business performance.

Leadership with a Global Strategy

The first major businesses in a region often provide the leadership and platform for the community's development and growth. Their industrial base and character shape the prospects for those who come later and provide connections between the community and the wider economy.

In the Upstate, foreign investment began in Spartanburg, and the foundation was large textile companies. When Roger Milliken, CEO of Milliken & Company,

moved the company's headquarters and his family from
New York to Spartanburg in 1954, he set in motion a
number of forces that eventually brought economic
strength to the region as a global center. Milliken saw the
need to compete with inexpensive imports by moderniz-
ing equipment and raising skill levels to improve quality
and bring labor costs under control. In the late 1950s, he
started urging German and Swiss manufacturers that
supplied the textile industry to set up shop in Spartanburg close to their customers. For many local residents,
the arrival of Milliken and other northern executives was
the first "foreign" influence in the area. It highlighted the
need for improvements in education and brought cosmopolitan attitudes even before the foreign companies
arrived.

Richard E. Tukey, executive director of the Spartanburg Area Chamber of Commerce from 1951 until his
death in 1979, was the driving force behind efforts to
attract foreign investment to the Upstate. Tukey was a
visionary who realized that opportunities had to be culti-
vated for a declining textile industry that was the area's
principal economic base. People in Spartanburg were
open to foreign investment because the alternatives were
poor jobs in textile or poultry plants or no jobs at all.
Tukey went overseas to textile machinery shows to find
investors and developed a wide network of business contacts in Europe. In 1965, he helped establish the U.S. base
for Menzel of Germany in just four days, including locating housing for the plant manager and finding someone
to write articles of incorporation for the company. When
Kurt Zimmerli, CEO of Zima, first explored moving to
the area, Tukey escorted him to banks and introduced
him to community leaders. Tukey was sometimes criticized for paying more attention to outside investors than

to local companies, but his persistence paid off in job growth that ultimately benefited local suppliers from construction crews to retailers.

Tukey was highly regarded by many civic leaders, and his allies included South Carolina's governors and lieutenant governors. He urged them to make the Upstate more attractive to Europeans by, for example, amending alcohol laws to make it easier to import wine. Tukey helped establish a variety of institutions that gave Spartanburg an international look, and he improved its cultural and educational offerings by initiating community events such as a German-style Oktoberfest and by working with local officials to create a state educational TV capability that was top-notch.

Reinforcing the Cycle of Development

The Upstate's business climate was hospitable to long-term outside investment, and the local work ethic was attractive to innovative companies. Spartanburg was the first of the two cities to catch the foreign wave, which started in the 1960s with a set of midsize companies that established their own greenfield sites rather than acquiring U.S. companies. Those companies stayed and expanded, often because their entrepreneurs were committed to growth in Spartanburg; some expatriates eventually became U.S. citizens and community leaders.

Several aspects of foreign investment in the area are noteworthy:

Industry Diversification Based on Core Skills. The textile industry provided a customer base, but the technical capabilities of the companies that moved into the area were not confined to one industry; they could be extended to many others.

Expansion and Upgrading. The foreign companies gradually expanded the region's functions, markets, and skills. Functions tended to expand from sales and service to manufacturing. Markets tended to expand from regional to North American to overseas. A regional office often became the North American headquarters. Initially, the companies transferred technology, standards, and skills from the foreign parent; eventually, many of the U.S. units outperformed the parents and educated them. According to a 1993 Greenville Chamber of Commerce survey of 87 foreign-owned companies, 80% had expanded since their arrival in the Upstate, and about 55% were planning a capital investment project in the next three years.

Entrepreneurship and Innovation. The first foreign companies were generally midsize. They had sent over individuals who could build new ventures from scratch and had granted them considerable autonomy to do so. U.S. operations were thus highly independent rather than subordinate branches of multinational giants; and foreign managers in the United States were entrepreneurs committed to growing the local business, not expatriates on short career rotations. Survival depended on a high degree of technological innovation.

Assimilation into the Local Culture. Companies generally sent over only a few foreigners, some of whom became U.S. citizens; the large number of U.S. hires gave the companies an American flavor. The first foreign company representatives were well-educated, English-speaking, cosmopolitan Europeans who could blend easily into the local population. Switzerland, Austria, and Germany—countries not intent on maintaining language purity or separatist traditions—were most often represented. Moreover, the original companies were not household names, not very visible, and not of particular interest to average citizens. But the new companies had a cultural style that complemented the local culture; they tended to sink roots and assimilate. According to local leaders, it took a long time for most people to realize just how many foreign companies there were in Spartanburg.

Among the first foreign companies to locate in the region was Rieter Machine Works of Winterthur, Switzerland. Rieter, whose first U.S. chief was a friend of Roger Milliken's, located its sales and service office in Spartanburg in 1959 because the U.S. textile industry was at the time 30% to 35% of its market. (It is now 20%.) Rieter gradually expanded into manufacturing, increasing its investment in South Carolina. Although the company found numerous differences between operating in Switzerland and in the United States—from measurement to quality standards—it found that it could blend American entrepreneurial flair with Swiss technical precision to achieve outstanding results. Ueli Schmid, the current CEO of Rieter in the United States, joined Rieter in Switzerland in 1970, moved to the States in 1980, and became a U.S. citizen.

As the Upstate proved hospitable to foreign investors, expansion from sales and service offices to manufacturing began. Menzel, from Bielefeld, Germany, established its sales office in Spartanburg in 1965 but soon realized it was more practical to build machinery there. It was the first European company to do so, and its presence paved the way for others. Menzel created an innovative material-handling system for large-roll batching used in plastics, fiberglass, rubber, and other applications besides textiles. Now three times its original size, it produces machinery in the United States that it does not build in Germany and derives less than 40% of its revenue from the textile industry.

Cosmopolitan entrepreneurs such as Hans Balmer came with the initial German and Swiss wave. In 1972 at the age of 25, Balmer was sent on a two-year assignment from Switzerland as Loepfe Brothers' U.S. representative. Instead of staying just two years, he married an American and, in 1985, founded his own business, Symtech. Now, with nearly $50 million in sales, Symtech uses the best models of supply-chain partnering to integrate manufacturing equipment from multiple suppliers for its customers. Balmer also has brought other foreign companies to Spartanburg, and he succeeded Kurt Zimmerli as international committee chair for the Spartanburg Area Chamber of Commerce.

An exception to the predominance of small and midsize companies in the initial foreign surge was the German chemical giant Hoechst. Hoechst traces its local origins to its 1967 joint venture with Hercules, a U.S. chemical company. (In 1987, Hoechst merged with Celanese to form Hoechst Celanese.) The company has both raw materials and fiber plants in the area; in the chemical plant alone, equity investment totals close to half a billion dollars. A truly global organization, Hoechst is a cosmopolitan force in Spartanburg. It gives its U.S. business relative autonomy but creates cross-cultural links through employee exchanges and technology transfers between Spartanburg and other worldwide facilities.

Besides bringing jobs to Spartanburg, Hoechst brought another important local leader: Paul Foerster. In 1967, Foerster moved to Spartanburg from Germany on a four-year contract to run the fibers facility. The contract was extended until his retirement in 1990. A cultural cross-fertilizer, Foerster turned Hoechst Celanese into an important charitable contributor to the region despite the absence of a charitable tradition in Germany. Today Foerster is honorary consul for Germany, liaison to Europe for South Carolina, past chairman of the Spartanburg Area Chamber of Commerce, and the one responsible for much of the international traffic through Spartanburg.

In the 1980s, attracting foreign investment became an explicit strategy for Greenville as well as for Spartanburg. Greenville has had a successful Headquarters Recruitment Program since 1985, and in 1993, 14 foreign companies announced that they would open new regional headquarters or expand existing offices in the city. By 1994, German companies still dominated in the Upstate with 65 of the region's 215 foreign companies; British companies were second with 43, and Japanese third with 29. Although there were only 16 French companies, employment in them was almost as great as in the German companies because of Michelin's large size. Foreign-owned service companies located in the region as well. Supermarket conglomerate Ahold of the Netherlands, a member of the European Retail Alliance, employs 4,000 people in the Upstate through its Bi-Lo chain, headquartered in Greenville.

Improving Training and Education

Good attitudes are not enough; workers' skills must meet international standards. For more than 30 years, the state has led a collaborative effort to provide outstanding technical training—a crucial factor in expanding high-wage manufacturing jobs in the Spartanburg-Greenville area.

Contrary to popular belief, low wages or tax incentives were not the primary reason the first foreign companies were attracted to South Carolina's Upstate region. Indeed, recent studies by James Hines of Harvard University's John F. Kennedy School of Government have shown that state and other local tax incentives play little or no role in where foreign companies locate their businesses in the United States. Foreign investors sometimes do decide to locate in a particular place in the United States if they will get tax credits at home for state tax payments, but generally, business factors play a larger role. South Carolina's principal attraction is the competence of its workforce.

The South Carolina State Board for Technical and Comprehensive Education offers free, customized technical training of prospective workers and supervisors to companies that bring new investment to the state. The board assigns staff to prepare manuals, interview workers, and teach classes based on technical requirements established by the company. The company is not obligated to hire any worker who completes the training, nor do workers have to accept any job offer. In some cases, the state will pay to send first-time line supervisors for training elsewhere, even in a foreign country. Training benefits apply to major facility expansions as well as to new sites. A related initiative is the Buy South Carolina program, which supports just-in-time inventory systems by finding local suppliers.

A network of 16 technical colleges runs the State Tech Special Schools, including Greenville Technical College, rated by *U.S. News & World Report* as one of the best technical schools in the country. Devised as a crash program to deal with economic desperation in 1961, the State Tech Special Schools are now a national model.

Since the network's inception, it has trained more than
145,000 workers for about 1,200 facilities, including more
than 30,000 for the textile industry, 34,000 for metalworking, and nearly 18,000 for electrical and electronic
machinery trades. In fiscal year 1992–1993, more than
6,400 people were trained for 121 companies, including
U.S. companies such as Tupperware and Perdue, at a
cost to the state of about $6.4 million. Companies also
can draw on training from the Quality Institute of Enterprise Development, a private nonprofit venture spun off
from the state's economic development board, which
partners with the Upstate's technical colleges, the University of South Carolina at Spartanburg, and local
chambers of commerce.

For German and Japanese companies with high technical and quality standards, such training is a major
incentive. Mita South Carolina, a Japanese toner pro-
ducer, used the State Tech Special Schools to build its
U.S. workforce after arriving in Greenville in 1991 to
manufacture for the North American market. Of its 150
current employees, only the top dozen managers are
Japanese (the heads of engineering and human resources
are Americans), and Japanese technicians were present
only to install machinery and troubleshoot when the
company started up. Some foreign managers want the
workforce to meet even higher standards, and German-
style apprenticeships are on the agenda.

The quality of public education also has improved
because of new business investment. Foreign companies
contributed by providing a sound tax base and a strong
vision of what education should be by setting high standards for workers' knowledge. But, according to educators, the presence of foreign companies was an excuse
for change, not a cause of it. Local interest and investment in educational reform have been consistent since

the 1950s, and in the 1980s the public and private sectors collaborated on an increase in the sales tax to provide for a 30% increase in school budgets. The state saw a rise of 128 points in average SAT scores, and Richard Riley, South Carolina's governor during this decade, went on to join the Clinton cabinet as the secretary of education. Although there were widespread improvements in the entire public education system, particular innovations came in the areas of language training, world geography, and world cultures. Spartanburg's District 7 high school was one of the first in the United States to offer advanced placement courses, and it continues to receive White House Achievement Awards—the only high school in the country said to have won three times. Greenville's South-side High School is the only high school in South Carolina, and one of a handful in the United States, that awards the International Baccalaureate Diploma. This program is modeled on the curricula of European schools and enables interested students to prepare to attend European universities.

International awareness and world-class capabilities are a priority also in the Upstate's colleges and universities. Skills in mathematics, science, computers, and technology are especially important because of the region's industrial base. However, educators also are upgrading language training, exchange programs, and internships abroad. For the latter, in particular, foreign companies are a key resource connecting local residents to many parts of the world.

Raising Standards Through Collaboration

Companies new to the Upstate discover strong cross-business and cross-sector collaboration that not only enhances business performance for both domestic and foreign companies but also strengthens the area's economy. Company executives comment repeatedly about strong networking, exchange of learning among businesses, as well as cooperation between businesses and government.

Strong, active chambers of commerce are catalysts for much of the cooperation, making the connections and mounting the programs that serve as the infrastructure for collaboration. The Spartanburg Area Chamber of Commerce has 1,800 members from 13 municipalities forming seven area councils. In 1989, it joined with the Spartanburg County Foundation—a charitable organization that supports community activities—and other groups to launch the Consensus Project, a community priority-setting activity based on a set of critical indicators of Spartanburg's community "health." The project began with about 75 leaders and eventually got feedback from many citizens. It has led to adult education, programs to prevent teenage pregnancy, and Leadership Spartanburg, a program that trains community leaders.

The Spartanburg Chamber offers programs that have directly improved business performance. It has a "vice president for quality"—an unusual office signifying the Chamber's activist role in industry and one that encourages innovative companies to learn from one another. In 1981, Milliken instituted a pioneering internal quality program, leading to a string of awards: the American Malcolm Baldrige National Quality Award, the British Quality Award, Canada Awards for Business Excellence, and the European Quality Award. Milliken was the first, and in some cases the only, fabric supplier to receive quality awards from General Motors, Ford, and Chrysler. With inspiration from Milliken, the Chamber's committee on quality launched the Quality in the Workplace program in 1984, very early in the U.S. total quality movement. In addition to educating numerous local companies, including those without their own quality or training staffs, the program extended the principles of quality to many nonprofits such as the United Way. The Greenville Chamber of Commerce—the state's largest, with 3,000 members—also facilitates collaboration. Companies exchange best-practice ideas, screen employees for jobs, encourage new companies to come to the area, solve one another's problems, and sometimes even lend one another staff. A monthly Chamber-sponsored manufacturers' discussion group helps with employee relations problems—something particularly beneficial to foreign companies employing a U.S. workforce—and serves as a job-finding network by circulating résumés and lists of names. When Sara Lee opened a plant in Greenville, Fuji's plant manager helped the company implement worker teams. At a Chamber "prospect" dinner, the representative of a smaller company being enticed to the area mentioned that the company could not afford a human resources function right away. Other manufacturers present, including Mita, volunteered to build a team of their own people to serve in the interim, to screen résumés and do the hiring.

Collaboration increasingly extends beyond political jurisdictions. A joint airport helped break the barrier between the two cities, and the wooing of BMW involved still more cooperation. Encouraged by a call from the governor's office, Spartanburg's and Greenville's hospital systems wrote a joint proposal about medical services in the area for BMW. The two cities compete for business investment, and there are continuing turf battles, especially among local politicians. But there also is a great deal of cooperative and overlapping activity; Greenville relishes Spartanburg's successes and vice versa. Behind these attitudes is more than the simple desire to be friendly. Leaders of the region increasingly acknowledge their shared fate as the pressures of growth and the stress on the existing infrastructure increase the demands on local resources. Many Spartanburg businesspeople call for greater cooperation between Spartanburg and Greenville, and between business and government, and even for the merger of the cities and counties into one metropolitan area. The Upstate's record of success in addressing the challenges of becoming a world-class maker will continue to be tested as the opportunities that have resulted from achieving global competence give rise to the challenges of sustaining growth.

Localizing the Global Economy

Ask people in Spartanburg and Greenville about the influence of foreign companies on their area, and they immediately turn to culture and cuisine: the annual International Festival; the Japanese tea garden, said to be the only authentic one in the United States outside the Japanese embassy in Washington; a surprising number of international organizations per capita; and many sister-city relationships. But the real impact has to do more with opening minds than with changing eating habits. Local residents have become more cosmopolitan, with extended horizons and higher standards.

The presence of foreign companies raised the adrenaline level of the business community, providing a new perspective that increased dissatisfaction with traditional practices and motivated people to improve. It was impossible to sustain sleepy local companies in an environment in which world-class companies came looking for better technology and skills. Business leaders and the workforce are now more aware of global standards. Suppliers to foreign companies credit them with raising standards to world-class levels. The main concern that residents have about foreign companies—a concern reluctantly but consistently voiced—is whether they will donate money or provide leadership to the community. Tensions often are framed in terms of community service, but the real problems come from local residents' suspicion that foreign companies that move capital into a community can all too easily move it out again and that locals will have no power to stop them. It takes time to educate foreign companies, many of them from countries whose social network is supported by government alone, about the United States' self-help, volunteer, and charitable traditions. But there are notable exceptions and increasing community support from foreign companies. Kurt Zimmerli, Paul Foerster, and Hans Balmer are frequently mentioned as examples of immigrants who became community leaders. Ueli Schmid secured a pool of money from Rieter to spend on discretionary local contributions. BMW makes its new facility available for community events. The self-reinforcing cycle of welcome succeeds as the Upstate's hospitable business climate creates an environment in which cosmopolitan leaders are willing to make deep commitments to the community.

Moreover, the locals' view is generally positive because foreign and outside investment has helped retain—and expand—homegrown companies in the area. For example, one of Spartanburg's oldest companies, Hersey Measurement, was saved by a joint venture between a U.S. company and a German company. Hersey was founded in 1859 to manufacture rotary pumps, bolts, and general machinery, and its new owners from Atlanta decided to keep the company in Spartanburg because of the excellent workforce. They expanded operations and built a new plant that doubled the size of its local facilities. Lockwood Greene Engineers, one of the oldest engineering-services companies in the United States, was reinvigorated by a German company after the failure of a management buyout. Metromont Materials, a leader in concrete, was acquired by a British company after large U.S. companies abandoned the industry. And locals report that even for residents not working at foreign-owned facilities, jobs are better paid and of better quality as a result of foreign investment in the region as a whole.

Becoming World-Class

The story of the Spartanburg-Greenville region illustrates what it takes to acquire the mind-set of the new world class. Cities and regions must become centers of globally relevant skills to enable local businesses and people to thrive. World-class businesses need concepts, competence, and connections, and world-class places can help grow these global assets by offering capabilities in innovation, production, or trade. Cities and regions will thrive to the extent that the businesses and people in them can develop better by being there rather than somewhere else.

To create this capability, communities need both magnets and glue. They must have magnets that attract a flow of external resources—new people or companies—to expand skills, broaden horizons, and hold up a comparative mirror against world standards. The flow might involve customers, outside investors, foreign companies, students, or business travelers. Communities also need social glue—a way to bring people together to define the common good, create joint plans, and identify strategies that benefit a wide range of people and organizations. In addition to the physical infrastructure that supports daily life and work—roads, subways, sewers, electricity, and communications systems—communities need an infrastructure for collaboration to solve problems and create the future. Community leaders must mount united efforts that enhance their connections to the global economy in order to attract and retain job-creating businesses whose ties reach many places.

And business leaders must understand how strong local communities can help them become more globally competitive. Businesses benefit from investing in a region's core skills. They derive advantages not only from creating company-specific resources but from establishing linkages outside the company as well. Local collaborations with international giants operating in their area can help smaller companies raise their standards and propel them into wider, more global markets. Leaders of large companies can strengthen their own competitiveness by developing a supportive environment in the primary places where they operate to ensure the availability of the highest-quality suppliers, workforce, living standards for their employees, and opportunities for partnership with local leaders.

Originally published in September–October 1995
Reprint R0308H

The End of Corporate Imperialism

C.K. PRAHALAD AND KENNETH LIEBERTHAL

Executive Summary

AS THEY SEARCH FOR GROWTH, multinational corporations will have no choice but to compete in the big emerging markets of China, India, Indonesia, and Brazil. But while it is still common to question how such corporations will change life in those markets, Western executives would be smart to turn the question around and ask how multinationals themselves will be transformed by these markets. To be successful, MNCs will have to rethink every element of their business models, the authors assert in this seminal HBR article from 1998.

During the first wave of market entry in the 1980s, multinationals operated with what might be termed an imperialist mind-set, assuming that the emerging markets would merely be new markets for their old products. But this mind-set limited their success: What is truly big and emerging in countries like China and India is a new consumer base comprising hundreds of millions of people. To tap into this huge opportunity, MNCs need to ask themselves five basic questions: Who is in the emerging middle class in these countries? How do the distribution networks operate? What mix of local and global leadership do you need to foster business opportunities? Should you adopt a consistent strategy for all your business units within one country? Should you take on local partners?

The transformation that multinational corporations must undergo is not cosmetic—simply developing greater sensitivity to local cultures will not do the trick, the authors say. To compete in the big emerging markets, multinationals must reconfigure their resources, rethink their cost structures, redesign their product development processes, and challenge their assumptions about who their top-level managers should be.

As THEY SEARCH FOR GROWTH, multinational corporations will have to compete in the big emerging markets of China, India, Indonesia, and Brazil. The operative word is "emerging." A vast consumer base of hundreds of millions of people is developing rapidly. Despite the uncertainty and the difficulty of doing business in markets that remain opaque to outsiders, Western MNCs will have no choice but to enter them. (See the exhibit "Market Size: Emerging Markets Versus the United States.")

During the first wave of market entry in the 1980s, MNCs operated with what might be termed an imperialist mind-set. They assumed that the big emerging markets were new markets for their old products. They foresaw a bonanza in incremental sales for their existing products or the chance to squeeze profits out of their sunset technologies. Further, the corporate center was seen as the sole locus of product and process innovation. Many multinationals did not consciously look at emerging markets as sources of technical and managerial talent for their global operations. As a result of this imperialist mind-set, multinationals have achieved only limited success in those markets.

Many corporations, however, are beginning to see that the opportunity big emerging markets represent will demand a new way of thinking. Success will require more than simply developing greater cultural sensitivity. The more we understand the nature of these markets, the more we believe that multinationals will have to rethink and reconfigure every element of their business models.

Market Size
Emerging Markets Versus the United States

Product	China	India	Brazil	United States
Televisions (million units)	13.6	5.2	7.8	23.0
Detergent (kilograms per person)	2.5	2.7	7.3	14.4
(million tons)	3.5	2.3	1.1	3.9
Shampoo ($ billions)	1.0	0.8	1.0	1.5
Pharmaceuticals ($ billions)	5.0	2.8	8.0	60.6
Automotive (million units)	1.6	0.7	2.1	15.5
Power (megawatt capacity)	236,542	81,736	59,950	810,964

So while it is still common today to question how corporations like General Motors and McDonald's will change life in the big emerging markets, Western executives would be smart to turn the question around. Success in the emerging markets will require innovation and resource shifts on such a scale that life within the multinationals themselves will inevitably be transformed. In short, as MNCs achieve success in those markets, they will also bring corporate imperialism to an end.

We would not like to give the impression that we think markets such as China, India, Brazil, and Indonesia will enjoy clear sailing. As Indonesia is showing, these markets face major obstacles to continued high growth; political disruptions, for example, can slow down and even reverse trends toward more open markets. But given the long-term growth prospects, MNCs will have to compete in those markets. Having studied in depth the evolution of India and China over the past 20 years, and having worked extensively with MNCs competing in these and other countries, we believe that there are five basic questions that MNCs must answer to compete in the big emerging markets:

- Who is the emerging middle-class market in these countries, and what kind of business model will effectively serve their needs?

- What are the key characteristics of the distribution networks in these markets, and how are the networks evolving?

- What mix of local and global leadership is required to foster business opportunities?

- Should the MNC adopt a consistent strategy for all its business units within one country?

• Will local partners accelerate the multinational's ability to learn about the market?

What Is the Business Model for the Emerging Middle Class?

What is big and emerging in countries like China and India is a new consumer base consisting of hundreds of millions of people. Starved of choice for over 40 years, the rising middle class is hungry for consumer goods and a better quality of life and is ready to spend. The emerging markets have entered a new era of product availability and choice. In India alone, there are 50 brands of toothpaste available today and more than 250 brands of shoes.

Consumers are experimenting and changing their choice of products rapidly. Indians, for example, will buy any product once, and brand switching is common. One survey found that Indian consumers tried on average 6.2 brands of the same packaged goods product in one year, compared with 2.0 for American consumers. But does this growth of consumer demand add up to a wealth of opportunity for the MNCs?

The answer is yes . . . but. Consider the constitution of the middle class itself. When managers in the West hear about the emerging middle class of India or China, they tend to think in terms of the middle class in Europe or the United States. This is one sign of an imperialist mind-set—the assumption that everyone must be just like us. True, consumers in the emerging markets today are much more affluent than they were before their countries liberalized trade, but they are not affluent by Western standards. This is usually the first big miscalculation that MNCs make.

When these markets are analyzed, moreover, they turn out to have a structure very unlike those of the West. Income levels that characterize the Western middle class would represent a tiny upper class of consumers in any of the emerging markets. Today the active consumer market in the big emerging markets has a three-tiered pyramid structure. (See the exhibit "The Market Pyramid in China, India, and Brazil.")

Consider India. At the top of the pyramid, in tier one, is a relatively small number of consumers who are responsive to international brands and have the income to afford them. Next comes tier two, a much larger group of people who are less attracted to international brands. Finally, at the bottom of the pyramid of consumers is tier three—a massive group that is loyal to local customs, habits, and often to local brands. Below that is another huge group made up of people who are unlikely to become active consumers anytime soon.

MNCs have tended to bring their existing products and marketing strategies to the emerging markets without properly accounting for these market pyramids. They end up, therefore, becoming high-end niche players.

The Market Pyramid in China, India, and Brazil

Purchasing Power (in U.S. dollars)		Population (in millions)		
		China	India	Brazil
tier 1	greater than $20,000	2	7	9
tier 2	$10,000 to $20,000	60	63	15
tier 3	$5,000 to $10,000	330	125	27
	less than $5,000	800	700	105

That's what happened to Revlon, for example, when it introduced its Western beauty products to China in 1976 and to India in 1994. Only the top tier valued and could afford the cachet of Revlon's brand. And consider Ford's recent foray into India with its Escort, which Ford priced at more than $21,000. In India, anything over $20,000 falls into the luxury segment. The most popular car, the Maruti Suzuki, sells for $10,000 or less. Fiat learned to serve that tier of the market in Brazil, designing a new model called the Palio specifically for Brazilians. Fiat is now poised to transfer that success from Brazil to India.

While it is seductive for companies like Ford to think of big emerging markets as new outlets for old products, a mind-set focused on incremental volume misses the real opportunity. To date, MNCs like Ford and Revlon have either ignored tier two of the pyramid or conceded it to local competitors. But if Ford wants to be more than a small, high-end player, it will have to design a robust and roomy $9,000 car to compete with Fiat's Palio or with a locally produced car.

Tailoring products to the big emerging markets is not a trivial task. Minor cultural adaptations or marginal cost reductions will not do the job. Instead, to overcome an implicit imperialism, companies must undergo a fundamental rethinking of every element of their business model.

RETHINKING THE PRICE/PERFORMANCE EQUATION

Consumers in big emerging markets are getting a fast education in global standards, but they often are unwilling to pay global prices. In India, an executive in a multinational food-processing company told us the story of a man in Delhi who went to McDonald's for a hamburger.

He didn't like the food or the prices, but he liked the ambience. Then he went to Nirula's, a successful Delhi food chain. He liked the food and the prices there, but he complained to the manager because Nirula's did not have the same pleasant atmosphere as McDonald's. The moral of the story? Price/performance expectations are changing, often to the consternation of both the multinationals and the locals. McDonald's has been forced to adapt its menu to local tastes by adding vegetable burgers. Local chains like Nirula's have been pushed to meet global standards for cleanliness and ambience.

Consumers in the big emerging markets are far more focused than their Western counterparts on the price/performance equation. That focus tends to give low-cost local competitors the edge in hotly contested markets. MNCs can, however, learn to turn this price sensitivity to their advantage.

Philips Electronics, for example, introduced a combination video-CD player in China in 1994. Although there is virtually no market for this product in Europe or the United States, the Chinese quickly embraced it as a great two-for-one bargain. More than 15 million units have been sold in China, and the product seems likely to catch on in Indonesia and India. Consumers in those countries see the player as good value for the money.

RETHINKING BRAND MANAGEMENT

Armed with their powerful, established brands, multinationals are likely to overestimate the extent of Westernization in the emerging markets and the value of using a consistent approach to brand management around the world.

In India, Coca-Cola overvalued the pull of its brand among the tier-two consumers. Coke based its advertising strategy on its worldwide image and then watched the advantage slip to Pepsi, which had adopted a campaign that was oriented toward the Indian market. As one of Coke's senior executives recently put it in the *Wall Street Journal,* "We're so successful in international business that we applied a tried-and-true formula...and it was the wrong formula to apply in India."

It took Coke more than two years to get the message, but it is now repositioning itself by using local heroes, such as popular cricket players, in its advertising. Perhaps more important, it is heavily promoting a popular Indian brand of cola—Thums Up—which Coke bought from a local bottler in 1993 only to scorn it for several years as a poor substitute for the Real Thing.

RETHINKING THE COSTS OF MARKET BUILDING

For many MNCs, entering an emerging market means introducing a new product or service category. But Kellogg, for example, found that introducing breakfast cereals to India was a slow process because it meant creating new eating habits. Once the company had persuaded Indians to eat cereal, at great expense, local competitors were able to ride on Kellogg's coattails by introducing breakfast cereals with local flavors. As a result, Kellogg may discover in the long run that it paid too high a price for too small a market. Sampling, celebrity endorsements, and other forms of consumer education are expensive: Regional tastes vary, and language barriers can create difficulties. India, for example, has more than a dozen major languages and pronounced cultural differences across regions.

Multinationals would do well to rethink the costs of building markets. Changing developed habits is difficult and expensive. Providing consumers with a new product that requires no reeducation can be much easier. For example, consider the rapid adoption of pagers in China. Because telephones are not widely available there, pagers have helped fill the void as a means of one-way communication.

RETHINKING PRODUCT DESIGN

Even when consumers in emerging markets appear to want the same products as are sold elsewhere, some redesign is often necessary to reflect differences in use and distribution. Because the Chinese use pagers to send entire messages—which is not how they were intended to be used—Motorola developed pagers capable of displaying more lines of information. The result: Motorola encountered the enviable problem of having to scramble to keep up with exploding demand for its product.

In the mid-1980s, a leading MNC in telecommunications began exporting its electronic switching system to China for use in the phone system. The switching system had been designed for the company's home market, where there were many customers but substantial periods when the phones were not in use. In China, on the other hand, there were very few phones, but they were in almost constant use. The switching system, which worked flawlessly in the West, simply couldn't handle the load in China. Ultimately, the company had to redesign its software.

Distribution can also have a huge impact on product design. A Western maker of frozen desserts, for example, had to reformulate one of its products not because of differences in consumers' tastes but because the refrigerators in most retail outlets in India weren't cold enough to store the product properly. The product had been designed for storage at minus 15 degrees centigrade, but the typical retailer's refrigerator operates at minus four degrees. Moreover, power interruptions frequently shut down the refrigerators.

RETHINKING PACKAGING

Whether the problem is dust, heat, or bumpy roads, the distribution infrastructure in emerging markets places special strains on packaging. One glass manufacturer, for example, was stunned at the breakage it sustained as a result of poor roads and trucks in India.

And consumers in tiers two and three are likely to have packaging preferences that are different from consumers in the West. Single-serve packets, or sachets, are enormously popular in India. They allow consumers to buy only what they need, experiment with new products, and conserve cash at the same time. Products as varied as detergents, shampoos, pickles, cough syrup, and oil are sold in sachets in India, and it is estimated that they make up 20% to 30% of the total sold in their categories. Sachets are spreading as a marketing device for such items as shampoos in China as well.

RETHINKING CAPITAL EFFICIENCY

The common wisdom is that the infrastructure problems in emerging markets—inefficient distribution systems, poor banking facilities, and inadequate logistics—will require companies to use more capital than in Western markets, not less. But that is the wrong mind-set. Hindustan Lever, a subsidiary of Unilever in India, saw a low-cost Indian detergent maker, Nirma, become the largest branded detergent maker in the world over a seven-year period by courting the tier-two and tier-three markets. Realizing that it could not compete by making marginal changes, Hindustan Lever rethought every aspect of its business, including production, distribution, marketing, and capital efficiency.

Today Hindustan Lever operates a $2 billion business with effectively zero working capital. Consider just one of the practices that makes this possible. The company keeps a supply of signed checks from its dealers. When it ships an order, it simply writes in the correct amount for the order. This practice is not uncommon in India. The Indian agribusiness company, Rallis, uses it with its 20,000 dealers in rural India. But this way of doing things is unheard of in Unilever's home countries—the United Kingdom and the Netherlands.

Hindustan Lever also manages to operate with minimal fixed capital. It does so in part through an active program of supplier management; the company works with local entrepreneurs who own and manage plants whose capacity is dedicated to Hindustan Lever's products. Other MNCs will find that there is less need for vertical integration in emerging markets than they might think. Quality suppliers can be located and developed. Their lower overhead structure can help the MNCs gain a competitive cost position. Supply chain management is an important tool for changing the capital efficiency of a multinational's operations.

Rather than concede the market, Hindustan Lever radically changed itself and is today successfully competing against Nirma with a low-cost detergent called Wheel. The lesson learned in India has not been lost on Unilever. It is unlikely to concede tier-two and tier-three markets in China, Indonesia, or Brazil without a fight.

How Does the Distribution System Work?

One of the greatest regrets of multinational executives, especially those we spoke with in China, was that they had not invested more in distribution before launching their products. Access to distribution is often critical to success in emerging markets, and it cannot be taken for granted. There is no substitute for a detailed understanding of the unique characteristics of a market's distribution system and how that system is likely to evolve.

Consider the differences between China and India. Distribution in China is primarily local and provincial. Under the former planned economy, most distribution networks were confined to political units, such as counties, cities, or provinces. Even at present there is no real national distribution network for most products. Many MNCs have gained access to provincial networks by creating joint ventures. But these are now impediments to the creation of the badly needed national network; Chinese joint-venture partners protect their turf. This gap between the MNCs' need for a national, cost-effective distribution system and the more locally oriented goals of their partners is creating serious tensions. We expect that many joint ventures formed originally to allow multinationals to have market and distribution access will be restructured because of this very issue during the next five to seven years.

In India, on the other hand, individual entrepreneurs have already put together a national distribution system in a wide variety of businesses. Established companies such as Colgate-Palmolive and Godrej in personal care, Hindustan Lever in packaged goods, Tatas in trucks, Bajaj in scooters—the list is long—control their own distribution systems. Those systems take the form of long-standing arrangements with networks of small-scale distributors throughout the country, and the banking network is part of those relationships. Many of the established packaged goods companies reach more than 3 million retail outlets—using trains, trucks, bullock-drawn carts, camels, and bicycles. And many companies claim to service each one of those outlets once a week.

Nevertheless, any MNC that wants to establish its own distribution system in India inevitably runs up against significant obstacles and costs. Ford, for example, is trying to establish a new, high-quality dealer network to sell cars in India. To obtain a dealership, each prospective dealer is expected to invest a large amount of his own money and must undergo special training. In the long haul, Ford's approach may prove to be a major source of advantage to the company, but the cost in cash and managerial attention of building the dealers' network will be substantial.

Ironically, the lack of a national distribution system in China may be an advantage. MNCs with patience and ingenuity can more easily build distribution systems to suit their needs, and doing so might confer competitive advantages. As one manager we talked to put it, "The trick to sustained, long-term profitability in China lies not in technology or in savvy advertising or even in low pricing but rather in building a modern distribution system." Conceivably, China may see consolidation of the retail market earlier than India.

The Chinese and Indian cases signal the need for MNCs to develop a market-specific distribution strategy. In India, MNCs will have to determine who controls national distribution in order to distinguish likely partners from probable competitors. In China, multinationals seeking national distribution of their products must consider the motivations of potential partners before entering relationships that may frustrate their intentions.

Will Local or Expatriate Leadership Be More Effective?

Leadership of a multinational's venture in an emerging market requires a complex blend of local sensitivity and global knowledge. Getting the balance right is critical but never easy. MNCs frequently lack the cultural understanding to get the mix of expatriate and local leaders right.

Expatriates from the multinational's host country play multiple roles. They transfer technology and management practices. They ensure that local employees understand and practice the corporate culture. In the early stages of market development, expatriates are the conduits for information flow between the multinational's corporate office and the local operation. But while headquarters staffs usually recognize the importance of sending information to the local operation, they tend to be less aware that information must also be received from the other direction. Expatriates provide credibility at headquarters when they convey information, especially information concerning the adaptations the corporation must make in order to be successful in the emerging market. Given these important roles, the large number of expatriates in China—170,000 by one count—is understandable.

Every multinational operation we observed in China had several expatriates in management positions. In India, by contrast, we rarely saw expatriate managers, and the few that we did see were usually of Indian origin. That's because among the big emerging markets, India is unique in that it has developed, over time, a cadre of engineers and managers. The Indian institutes of technology and institutes of management turn out graduates with a high degree of technical competence. Perhaps more important from the perspective of a multinational, Indian managers speak English fluently and seem adept at learning new corporate cultures. At the same time, they have a much better appreciation of local nuances and a deeper commitment to the Indian market than any expatriate manager could have.

Those seeming advantages may be offset, however, by two disadvantages. First, a management team of native-born managers may not have the same share of voice at corporate headquarters that expatriate managers have. Yet maintaining a strong voice is essential, given the difficulty most managers at corporate headquarters have in understanding the dynamics and peculiar requirements of operating in emerging markets. Second, the "soft technology" that is central to Western competitive advantage—the bundle of elements that creates a market-sensitive, cost-effective, dynamic organization—is hard to develop when the management team consists of people who have worked only briefly, if at all, in such an organization.

Several multinationals have sent expatriates of Chinese or Indian origin from their U.S. or European base back to their Chinese or Indian operations in order to convey the company's soft technology in a culturally sensitive way. But that strategy has not, in general, been successful. As one manager we spoke to noted, "Indians from the United States who are sent back as expatriates are frozen in time. They remember the India they left 20 years ago. They are totally out of sync. But they do not have the humility to accept that they have to learn." We heard the same sentiment echoed in China, both for Chinese-Americans and, less frequently, for Chinese who had obtained a higher education in the United States and then returned as part of a multinational management team.

Using American or West European expatriates during the early years of market entry can make sense, but this approach has its own set of problems. Cultural and language difficulties in countries like China and India typically limit expats' interaction with the locals as well as their effectiveness. In addition, the need to understand how to deal with the local political system, especially in China, makes long-term assignments desirable. It often takes an expatriate manager two years to get fully up to speed. From the company's perspective, it makes sense to keep that manager in place for another three years to take full advantage of what he or she has learned. But few Western expatriates are willing to stay in China that long; many feel that a long assignment keeps them out of the loop and may impose a high career cost. Multinationals, therefore, need to think about how to attract and retain high-quality expatriate talent, how to maintain expats' links to the parent company, and how to use and pass along expats' competencies once they move on to other assignments.

Is It Necessary to Present One Face?

Beyond the normal organizational questions that would exist wherever a company does business, there is a question of special importance in emerging markets: Do local political considerations require the multinational to adopt a uniform strategy for each of its business units operating in the country, or can it permit each unit to act on its own?

Again, the contrasts between China and India make clear why there is no one right answer to this question. In China, massive governmental interference in the economy makes a uniform country strategy necessary. The Chinese government tends to view the activities of individual business units as part of a single company's effort, and therefore concessions made by any one unit— such as an agreement to achieve a certain level of local sourcing—may well become requirements for the others. An MNC in China must be able to articulate a set of principles that conforms to China's announced priorities, and it should coordinate the activities of its various business units so that they resonate with those priorities.

But given the way most multinationals operate, presenting one face to China is very difficult. Business units have their own P&L responsibilities and are reluctant to lose their autonomy. Reporting lines can become overly complex. Although we observed many organizational approaches, not a single MNC we looked at is completely satisfied with its approach to this difficult issue.

Is it any wonder? Consider the life of one MNC executive we visited in China. As the head of his company's China effort, he has to coordinate with the company's regional headquarters in Japan, report to international headquarters in Europe, and maintain close contact with corporate headquarters in North America. He also has to meet with members of the Chinese government, with the MNC's business unit executives in China, and with the leaders of the business units' Chinese partners. Simply maintaining all of these contacts is extraordinarily taxing and time consuming.

There is somewhat less need to present one face to India. Since 1991, the Indian government has scaled back its efforts to shape what MNCs do in the country. Business units may therefore act more independently than would be appropriate in China. The strategy for India can be developed on a business-by-business basis. Nonetheless, the market is large and complex. National regulations are onerous, and state-level governments are still so different from one another that MNCs are well advised to develop knowledge that they can share with all their business units in India.

Do Partners Foster Valuable Learning?

In the first wave of market entry, multinationals used joint ventures extensively as a way not only to navigate through bureaucratic processes but also to learn about new markets. With few exceptions, however, joint ventures in emerging markets have been problematic. In some cases, executives of the multinationals mistakenly thought the joint venture would do their strategic thinking for them. In most cases, tensions in joint venture relationships have diverted management attention away from learning about the market.

One consistent problem is that each party enters the joint venture with very different expectations. One Chinese manager described the situation in terms of an old saying: "We are sleeping in the same bed with different dreams." The local partner sees the MNC as a source of technology and investment, and the multinational sees the partner as a means of participating in the domestic market.

When they come to an emerging market, multinationals are usually building manufacturing and marketing infrastructures, and they don't expect immediate returns. Local partners, however, often want to see short-term profit. This disparity of aims leads to enormous strain in the relationship. The costs associated with expatriate managers also become a bone of contention. Who controls what can be yet another source of trouble—especially when the domestic partner has experience in the business. And when new investment is needed to grow the business, local partners often are unable to bring in the matching funds, yet they resent the dilution of their holding and the ensuing loss of control.

MNCs are finally learning that their local partners often do not have adequate market knowledge. The experience of most local partners predates the emergence of real consumer markets, and their business practices can be archaic. As markets evolve toward greater transparency, as MNCs develop senior managers who understand how the system works, and as the availability of local talent increases, multinationals have less to gain by using intermediaries as a vehicle for learning.

The MNCs' need for local partners is already diminishing. In 1997, a consulting firm surveyed 67 companies invested in China and found that the percentage of their projects that became wholly foreign-owned enterprises grew steadily from 18% in 1992 to 37% in 1996. A passive partner that can provide a local face may still be important in some industries, but this is a very different matter from a joint venture.

Success Will Transform the Multinationals

As executives look for growth in the big emerging markets, they tend quite naturally to focus on the size of the opportunity and the challenges that lie ahead. Few stop to think about how success will transform their companies. But consider the magnitude of the changes we have been describing and the sheer size of the markets in question. Success in the big emerging markets will surely change the shape of the modern multinational as we know it today.

For years, executives have assumed they could export their current business models around the globe. That assumption has to change. Citicorp, for example, aims to serve a billion banking customers by 2010. There is no way Citicorp, given its current cost structure, can profitably serve someone in Beijing or Delhi whose net wealth is less than $5,000. But if Citicorp creates a new business model—rethinking every element of its cost structure—it will be able to serve not only average Chinese people but also inner-city residents in New York. In short, companies must realize that the innovation required to serve the large tier-two and tier-three segments in emerging markets has the potential to make them more competitive in their traditional markets— and therefore in all markets.

Over time, the imperialist assumption that innovation comes from the center will gradually fade away and die. Increasingly, as multinationals develop products better adapted to the emerging markets, they are finding that those markets are becoming an important source of innovation. Telecommunications companies, for example, are discovering that people in markets with no old technology to forget may accept technological changes faster. MNCs such as Texas Instruments and Motorola are assigning responsibility for software-oriented business development to their Indian operations. China has become such a significant market for video-CD players that the Chinese are likely to be major players in introducing the next round of video-CD standards around the world.

The big emerging markets will also have a significant influence on the product development philosophy of the MNCs. One major multinational recognized to its surprise that the Chinese have found a way of producing high-quality detergents with equipment and processes that cost about one-fifth of what the MNC spends. Stories like that can be repeated in a wide variety of businesses, including cement, textile machinery, trucks, and television sets.

As product development becomes decentralized, collaboration between labs in Bangalore, London, and Dallas, for example, will gradually become the rule, not the exception. New product introductions will have to take into consideration nontraditional centers of influence. Thus in the CD business at Philips, new product introductions, which previously occurred almost exclusively in Europe, now also take place in Shanghai and California.

As corporate imperialism draws to a close, multinationals will increasingly look to emerging markets for talent. India is already recognized as a source of technical talent in engineering, sciences, and software, as well as in some aspects of management. High-tech companies recruit in India not only for the Indian market but also for the global market. China, given its growth and its technical and management-training infrastructure, has not yet reached that stage, but it may well reach it in the not-too-distant future.

A major shift in geographical resources will take place within the next five years. Philips is already downsizing in Europe and reportedly employs more Chinese than Dutch workers. Over 40% of the market for Coca-Cola, Gillette, Lucent, Boeing, and GE Power Systems is in Asia. And in the last two years, ABB has shrunk its European workforce by more than 40,000 while adding 45,000 people in Asia.

In addition to these changes, an increasing percentage of the investment in marketing and in plant and equipment will go to the emerging markets. As those markets grow to account for 30% to 40% of capital invested—and even a larger percentage of market share and profits—they will attract much more attention from top management.

The importance of these markets will inevitably be reflected in the ethnic and national origin of senior management. At present, with a few exceptions such as Citicorp and Unilever, senior management ranks are filled with nationals from the company's home country. By the year 2010, however, the top 200 managers from around the world for any multinational will have a much greater cultural and ethnic mix.

How many of today's multinationals are prepared to accommodate 30% to 40% of their top team of 200 coming from China, India, and Brazil? How will that cultural mix influence decision making, risk taking, and team building? Diversity will put an enormous burden on top-level managers to articulate clearly the values and behaviors expected of senior managers, and it will demand large investments in training and socialization. The need for a single company culture will also become more critical as people from different cultures begin to work together. Providing the right glue to hold companies together will be a big challenge.

That challenge will be intensified by an impending power shift within multinationals. The end of corporate imperialism suggests more than a new relationship between the developed and the emerging economies. It also suggests an end to the era of centralized corporate power—embodied in the attitude that headquarters knows best—and a shift to a much more dispersed base of power and influence.

Consider the new patterns of knowledge transfer we are beginning to see. Unilever, for example, is transferring Indian managers with experience in low-cost distribution to China, where they will build a national distribution system and train Chinese managers. And it has transferred Indian managers with knowledge of tier-two markets to Brazil. The phenomenon of using managers from outside the home country to transfer knowledge is relatively new. It will grow over time to the point where the multinational becomes an organization with several centers of expertise and excellence.

Multinationals will be shaped by a wide variety of forces in the coming decades. The big emerging markets will be one of the major forces they come up against. And the effect will be nothing short of dramatic change on both sides. They will challenge each other to change for the better as a truly global economy takes shape in the twenty-first century. The MNCs will create a higher standard of products, quality, technology, and management practices. Large, opaque markets will gradually become more transparent. The process of transition to market economies will be evolutionary, uneven, and fraught with uncertainties. But the direction is no longer in question.

In order to participate effectively in the big emerging markets, multinationals will increasingly have to reconfigure their resource bases, rethink their cost structures, redesign their product development processes, and challenge their assumptions about the cultural mix of their top managers. In short, they will have to develop a new mind-set and adopt new business models to achieve global competitiveness in the postimperialist age.

Originally published in July–August 1998
Reprint R0308G

Turn Public Problems
to Private Account

RODMAN C. ROCKEFELLER

Executive Summary

MANY MANAGERS FACE increasing calls to invest corporate resources in charitable causes. How should executives balance a firm's very real economic imperative to maximize profitability with its hypothetical moral imperative to improve society?

To provide one answer, the author draws on his experience as president of an economic-development company, IBEC. Viewing profit as "an essential discipline and measurer of economic success" but not "the sole corporate goal," the company actively invested in social programs that met four criteria: They served a need of the local population; they required innovative approaches; they made sense on economic grounds; and they respected the social norms of the community. Such civic-minded efforts, the author argues in this prescient 1971 article, not only improve people's lives but also create the foundation for more affluent and dynamic markets—markets that ultimately produce greater profits for business.

For example, one of IBEC's earliest ventures was directed toward solving Venezuela's problems in retail food marketing. Many important items were unavailable at the small stores where people shopped. So in 1949, working with local partners, IBEC opened a supermarket. Supermarkets soon changed the food-buying habits of the nation, and the initiative helped alter patterns of food distribution and created the reliable demand needed to establish a host of local suppliers. Return on IBEC's investment, and that of its local partners, was most satisfactory, the author reports.

The road to meeting a public need—especially a major one—is rarely easy, the author says. But if management sizes up the need well, there is a good chance its new venture will survive under adversity.

ONE OF THE MORE CHALLENGING problems facing American businessmen is how we and our corporations can relate to some of today's pressing societal problems without compromising our responsibilities to maintain profitable growth. Certainly many of us are deeply and sincerely concerned with the social and environmental questions that confront our nation. We have demonstrated this concern repeatedly by giving selflessly of our time and effort to help create organizations like the National Alliance of Businessmen and the Urban Coalition, or to help manage the many continuing experienced efforts such as the Salvation Army, the Interracial Council for Business Opportunity, and the National

Urban League, designed to be responsive to current national economic and social needs.

On a local level, community officials look to us for leadership in fighting the malaise that grips our nation's cities. Corporate executives serve on countless boards, study groups, and commissions, earnestly seeking ways to improve the quality of life around us.

So great, in fact, is our sense of commitment that more executive time is being devoted to this type of "extracurricular" activity than ever before. But until quite recently the overwhelming part of this activity stemmed from a personal rather than a corporate commitment. We sought to involve ourselves with societal problems out of a sense of duty as private citizens. The leadership role was thrust on us either by design or default, because of proven abilities "to get things done"—qualities essential to the implementation of beneficial change.

As a result, many of us operate in two distinct worlds. During most of the day, we wear corporate hats, conducting the affairs of the enterprise and doing it with a high degree of efficiency and profit. At other times, we employ these same talents in the service of the community—but as individuals acting outside the mainstream of our primary business concerns.

I don't mean to imply that we are schizophrenic about this. After all, the executive who works weekends for a project of the Interracial Council is the same man who helps set policy in a manufacturing or service company. But we do seem to have done more to help solve social problems in our capacity as private individuals than in our capacity as members of corporate teams. In fact, when wearing our corporate hats we sometimes seem reluctant to involve our corporations in social problems because of feelings about our responsibilities to shareholders.

Pressures and Questions

All this gives rise to a problem: Today, society is demanding a greater commitment by business to socioeconomic tasks. There is growing and ever more vocal insistence that we in management should commit corporate resources, as well as our personal ones, to the battle against the social and environmental ills that plague us, many of which are alleged to be the inadvertent results of industrial successes in the past. Understandably, the demands make many of us uneasy. Privately we may concede that such an extension of the corporation's role could be highly beneficial to society. But may we not betray our mandate as corporate managers if we push our enterprises in these new directions? Do we have a right to do so? If so, where should we draw the line?

These are not simple questions, nor can they be answered in the same way for all of industry. There are enormous contrasts between industries and between companies within the same industry, with the result that what is practical in one case may be completely impractical in another. For instance, it would not make sense to draw the same line for both an apparel company and a transportation company, with the latter closely involved on a day-to-day basis with state and local governments, and the former not involved much with government at all. In one case, political considerations are a major factor; in the other, they are not—and that has a major bearing on what the companies are able to do as well as on what they can reasonably be expected to do.

In this article, therefore, I shall not try to prescribe for U.S. business in general but to describe how a company has decided it can best meet socioeconomic needs both in this country and overseas. The company is the organization with which I am associated, International Basic Economy Corporation (IBEC). We have long operated in economic sectors such as agribusiness, where demand and supply are political as well as economic questions, with the result that public needs become an important part of the decision-making process.

While IBEC's approach should not be used as a blueprint for other companies, its experience will, I hope, prove useful to many business executives. It demonstrates how far a company can go in meeting socioeconomic needs, given the right conditions, and illustrates some important principles to follow in going about that task.

Leadership at a Profit

First, let me summarize the ideas held by the founders and management of IBEC about the role of the corporation in socioeconomic affairs:

- If the many problems faced by our society could be attacked from an entrepreneurial as well as from a community action or philanthropic approach, society and business would benefit immeasurably. But the private sector cannot and should not undertake to meet all of society's needs. Many vital functions and services must be provided on the basis of need rather than ability to pay.

- Business will profit by assuming a more aggressive leadership role as an innovative force capable of exercising social judgment, consciously initiating change, and shaping the overall environment. Such an approach means that profit is valued as an essential discipline and measurer of economic success, not as the sole corporate goal. We need to enlarge the dimensions of corporate purpose so as to recognize that interest in sound, long-range developmental investment brings great common benefits, and hence common support.

These principles guided the founders of IBEC when it was formed 23 years ago. IBEC's founders wanted to invest profitably in the developing nations in such a way as to improve the social and economic conditions of those nations. They were so resolved to test the validity of their philosophy that they used it as the preamble of the company's proposed draft for the certificate of incorporation to be filed with the State of New York:

> *"We, the undersigned, desiring in association with others to promote the economic development of various parts of the world, to increase the production and availability of goods, things, and services useful to the lives or livelihood of their peoples, and thus to better their standards of living, and believing that these aims can be furthered through a corporation dedicated to their fulfillment and employing scientific and modern methods and techniques...."*

Among outsiders there was considerable skepticism about such a philosophy then—and there still is today. In reply, I can only submit evidence that it is working successfully for IBEC. We have made money by meeting human needs in an efficient and businesslike way. Over the past ten years, for example, our total revenue has nearly tripled, and our stockholders' equity has more than doubled. Last year, we earned $1.72 per share on a total revenue of $256 million, and the results so far this year lead us to expect even further improvement.

It is quite true that we have had our share of failures as well as successes. But, in retrospect, we can identify the reasons for both and discern the combination of elements that led to success. In the case of IBEC, success in operations has usually depended on a combination of four guidelines. We have found it important to:

1. attempt to identify a human need in a particular market, usually a developing area;

2. try to develop fresh, innovative ways to meet that need in that market;

3. subject any concrete proposal to a searching analysis in order to determine if it will meet standard financial criteria of a workable business enterprise, and if local management is capable of success; and

4. satisfy ourselves that the new venture does not violate the cultural, social, and economic values of the people for whom it is intended.

Almost without exception, failures have resulted from our neglect of one or more of these guidelines. However, when all four of them have been duly observed, we have been generally rewarded by success.

In the pages that follow I shall illustrate each of these guidelines with cases from our experience. A final example, taken from IBEC's operations in the United States, will illustrate the total approach.

Identify a Need

One of IBEC's earliest ventures was directed toward solving the retail food marketing problems that existed in Venezuela. Before we entered the scene, food marketing was done through small so-called bodegas, or mom-and-pop corner stores. As a rule, these kept poorly displayed, inadequate stocks of merchandise. Turnover tended to be slow and margins high. In addition, many important items were not available locally or, if they were, had to be imported at high cost. Taken together, these factors penalized the average consumer by causing unnecessarily high prices for food that was available within the country, and by effectively depriving him of items that were not.

We felt that the establishment of efficient patterns of food distribution that would result in lower prices to the buyer, and the encouragement of local entrepreneurs to become domestic suppliers, were clearly in the interests of Venezuelan national development. The technique of supermarkets was already well proven in other areas. Why not bring the technique to Venezuela?

In 1949, in Maracaibo, working with local partners, IBEC opened the first supermarket in a chain that is known today as C.A. Distribuidora de Alimentos (CADA). Since that time, our supermarkets have helped to change the food buying habits of the nation. In addition, we have helped to alter patterns of food distribution and have created the assured demand needed to establish a host of local suppliers. Today, our 35 supermarkets are a familiar sight throughout the country. For millions of families, the concept of one-stop, self-service, low-margin shopping, entirely unknown 20 years ago, is now a familiar and accepted pattern. Return on our investment, and that of our local partners, has been most satisfactory.

The road to meeting a public need—especially a major one—is rarely easy. But if management sizes up the need well, the chances improve that its new venture will survive in adversity. Let us return to IBEC's supermarket venture. (Here we will also see some of the other guidelines illustrated.)

During the early years of this operation, we were forced to weather fairly widespread and sharp criticism, especially from small shop owners, who feared they would be priced out of business. While it is true that our large-volume buying capabilities and more efficient management techniques permitted us to lower food prices by about 8% to 10%, we did not smother local competition. Quite the contrary: Our presence seemed to provide many small store owners with a fresh stimulus. Their displays were made more attractive, storefronts were modernized, and credit sales were encouraged. Instead of languishing, the neighborhood corner store in Venezuela took on a new vigor, and the more resourceful owners represented, as they still do, an extremely healthy competition.

The impact made by the supermarkets on small stores is illustrated by a much-repeated (and probably apocryphal) story:

A bodega owner was met by a neighbor at the CADA checkout while the owner was unloading an immensely full basket of groceries. When asked what she was doing shopping in the competitor's store, the owner answered, "I am getting all I can of this low-cost food before these crazy people go out of business."

Today, 98% of food sales in Venezuela are in national hands, including three very vigorous supermarket competitors who have very successfully copied our methods. We consider this development a decided compliment and an unmistakable proof of our success, for no one emulates a failure. In any event, it has served to bear out our earlier conviction that there was a genuine need for modern, efficient food retailing operations in Venezuela and further strengthens our belief in the principle that many human needs can be effectively met by highly motivated, profit-oriented private enterprise.

Develop New Methods

Once a need is identified, it is usually important to develop innovative ways of meeting it. Our experience in Venezuela again offers a good illustration.

In 1948, IBEC formed a company known as Industria Lactea de Carabobo C.A. (INLACA). This was done with local partners. The purpose of INLACA was to bring pasteurized fresh milk at reasonable prices to the Venezuelan market. From the very beginnings of our operations in that country, it has been obvious that Venezuela suffered from a shortage of sanitary milk. Only 13% of national consumption came from local herds. The remainder was based on reconstituted powdered milk that was imported. This situation made no sense whatsoever, because enormous stretches of central and western Venezuela, covered with tall, natural grasses, were ideal for cattle grazing.

One of the difficulties lay with the native cattle. Not only were they poor milkers, but their milk production fluctuated greatly because of uncontrolled breeding, disease, the danger of flooding in the wet season, and lack of food in the dry season. Clearly, some incentive had to be found that would persuade Venezuelan milk producers to become better farmers and upgrade the quality of their product.

Not surprisingly, the best incentive to be found was effective, dependable demand for milk. We created confidence in the retail product through quality. It was a simple enough concept, but it had never before been tried in Venezuela. The farmers responded with serious attempts to upgrade their operations; in some cases, our company aided them in this effort. Other factors also contributed to a general improvement in local production. The government, for example, moved on a broad scale to support the infant dairy industry by introducing new methods of breeding and by importing new strains of cattle.

While it would be presumptuous for us to claim that we created the dairy industry in Venezuela single-handedly, it is nevertheless true that, by our example and our commercial success, we acted as a powerful catalyst for change and were instrumental in bringing effective techniques to bear on important social and economic problems. The formula was so successful that in a very short time not only did we find ourselves competing vigorously with others who had entered the industry, but Venezuela found itself with a seasonal surplus of fresh milk instead of the costly deficit it had endured.

We are on the lookout for businesses which by their nature are beneficial to the public in general. For this reason our acquisition policy is oriented toward products and companies which serve important "basic" needs. For example:

Our subsidiary, Arbor Acres Farm, occupies a position of worldwide leadership in the poultry breeding industry. Through its extensive genetic research capability, the company has been a key force in developing new commercial sources of protein where little had existed before. A few facts reveal the impact that such a venture can have.

When Arbor Acres first began breeder operations in Argentina in 1961, only a fraction of the poultry consumed in that country was commercially produced. As a result, production was inefficient, and the cost of this important source of high-protein food was extravagantly high. Within a short time, the company was able to demonstrate that its breeds and modern poultry management techniques could raise a meat bird to market in eight and a half weeks as compared with 13 weeks in the past—and do it at about one-third of the cost of the techniques then employed.

Egg production, too, was correspondingly improved in Argentina, rising from an average of 120 eggs per year per hen to an average of 205, using Arbor Acres breeds. In addition, the vaccination and disease-eradication procedures which the United States developed and introduced have now become well established in Argentina (and other South American countries), thus providing a graphic illustration of how technologies can be successfully transferred.

Analyze Profitability

The third guideline for successful operations is that the project under consideration must be subjected to a searching financial analysis. Does it meet the standard financial criteria of a workable business enterprise?

To illustrate how IBEC has applied this rule, let us turn to the field of savings and capital supply. Since the formation of a national capital market is essential to the orderly development of an industrial base that is not externally controlled, we have been concerned with the marshaling of local capital in order to encourage local industry.

We were among the first to form mutual funds in Latin America. One of the more successful funds is in Brazil. This fund has reached a total of 36,000 shareholders and managed assets in excess of $20 million, the overwhelming majority of this sum invested in Brazilian companies. Two years ago, the fund was combined with a private investment banking company to form Brazil's leading diversified investment banking and credit institution. It remains a potent force in the national capital market. Total managed assets of the combined company are in excess of $200 million. Majority control is held by Brazilians.

But perhaps IBEC's most dramatic impact in the area of capital mobilization was in Spain, where, four years ago, the company founded a fund with managed assets of approximately $800,000. At the end of 1969, the mutual fund had become the largest in Spain, with managed assets of $93 million, more than 30,000 investors, and a portfolio made up entirely of Spanish securities. This sizable concentration of capital did not come primarily, as one might expect, from the larger cities. On the contrary, over 60% of the invested funds were drawn from the savings of individuals living in the rural areas of the country. This meant that we were tapping a fresh source of capital that had never before been put to work on behalf of Spanish national development.

However, well before we committed ourselves to our mutual fund activity in Spain, we subjected the idea to careful scrutiny in an attempt to see if the project made business sense. The economy and demography of the country were thoroughly analyzed by members of the feasibility team, for it had to be clear that this relatively new undertaking would be profitable as well as a contribution to the country's social and economic development. As a result, a series of reports and studies was compiled. One of them included a prefeasibility-study checklist that contained no less than 88 separate questions that had to be satisfactorily answered before we proceeded. These ranged from an exploration of the size and influence of various existing financial institutions to the reliability of local communications facilities.

A preliminary assessment revealed that a massive industrialization program initiated by the government in 1950 was beginning to take hold. By 1960, real growth in GNP was in evidence, inflation was being curbed, and with an influx of foreign tourists, a favorable balance of trade had been established.

Furthermore, the public appeared to be able to generate savings. Out of a population of about 30 million, some 10 million had accounts in Spanish banks with assets totaling $2.2 billion. It was estimated that 3 million of these savers would be potential investors in a mutual fund since the annual interest rate from savings institutions averaged only 2%. A further study of income distribution indicated that a sizable proportion of the working population would benefit from such a fund, and of these, by far the greatest number were members of the middle and lower classes, people who were earning less than $120 per month.

Previously there had been little participation in mutual funds by the public, since funds were used as private holding companies by the banks. Once enabling legislation was passed by the government, it was decided, on the basis of our studies, that a mutual fund could be operated successfully in Spain through the mobilization of lower-income capital.

Observe Social Norms

Finally, it is very important to operate within the framework of cultural, social, and economic values held by the people who will benefit from the project. To see how this guideline works, let us turn to one of IBEC's U.S. projects.

Not long ago, we decided to enter the middle- to low-cost housing market in the rural and suburban areas of the South. We wanted to meet the needs of the emerging black middle class, whose housing demands had not been met. For our pilot project, initiated early in 1970, we selected Spartanburg, South Carolina, where we could see a clearly identifiable market of the type described. We hoped our program would be the beginning of a major effort in the Spartanburg area, with considerable sales and marketing potential. (A large majority of the 200 homes on this first project are being built under the Federal Housing Administration's Section 235 program, which allows a family earning between $5,000 and $8,000 a year to purchase a home that can be worth as much as $18,000.)

How was the venture shaped to the needs of the individuals we meant to serve? Before even so much as a blade of grass was moved at the project site, a two-man team, one an architect, the other a sociologist, conducted in-depth interviews in an attempt to assess the lifestyles of prospective customers. The desires were many and resulted in important modifications. I doubt we would have made these changes had we not taken the trouble to inquire. The majority of intended buyers were black families; yet construction in the area had been traditionally in the hands of white developers and builders, who built houses for the black community that mirrored middle-class white preferences and desires, which were often different from those of black families.

The study paid us handsome dividends. During the first two weeks that model homes were open for inspection, we sold houses at the rate of two a day.

Meeting All the Tests

Now let us look at a case example showing how all four of the guidelines aided IBEC's management in conceiving and directing a major project.

Of all the examples I could give in this article, perhaps none more clearly illustrates the business opportunities to be derived from converting human problems into realistic markets than does IBEC's experience in building homes for American Indians. For years, it has been recognized that American Indians, both on and off reservations, live in unspeakable poverty and in housing so deplorable that it undermines their health and dulls their ambition.

We determined to see if we could do something to solve the housing problem. We were told initially that it was a waste of time to build homes for Indians. They would not "appreciate it," we were informed, and they would not take care of their property once they moved in. In a year or so, their once-new houses would revert to the shanties they had left.

The most interesting phrase in this litany of objection, it seemed to us, was the reference to building homes "for Indians." What if, instead of building homes *for* Indians, we built homes *with* Indians? Would they then take a pride in ownership because they had participated in the effort? Indeed, would they even be willing to work with us? No one knew the answers, but we were willing to experiment.

Fortunately, there existed at that time a legal governmental vehicle through which the project could be realized. This was a joint memorandum developed by the Public Health Service, the Public Housing Authority, and

the Bureau of Indian Affairs in 1964. It proposed a
Mutual Self-Help Housing Project for Indians; in this
project, Public Housing would provide the loan funds,
the Bureau would provide staffing services, and Public
Health would provide water facilities for Indian projects.
In the spring of 1967, the Cherokee Nation invited us
to Talequah, Oklahoma, for discussions. Getting to know
the Indian tribal authorities was a time-consuming
affair. Establishing our credibility was essential. We proposed a pilot project of 30 units. The key to success, we
realized, was full cooperation by the Indian families
themselves.

Under the terms of the agreement, each family was
called on to contribute approximately one acre of land,
which was arbitrarily valued at $250. In addition, each
family committed its members to a total of 500 hours of
work on the project. To make this work contribution
even more acceptable, the 500 hours of work were trans-
lated into an amount of physical work to be done. It
became unnecessary, therefore, to require exactly 500
hours of work by time measurement.

The participants were able to make their contribution
in terms of work finished and to stretch their effort over
the life of the project, working on specific, agreed-upon
project steps. The need to produce this work on time as
the project progressed was understood by all and indeed
served as a stimulant to the performance of the work.
The 500 hours, known as "sweat equity," was valued at
$1,500 and was considered the family's down payment
toward the purchase price. After completion, the family
was to make monthly maintenance payments of between
$9 and $22, depending on its income and ability to pay,
for a total period of approximately 18 years. After that,

the title to the house would belong free and clear to the Indian family.

The families cooperated magnificently and enthusiastically. They were divided into teams for training in various semiskilled functions. They worked together on each other's houses under our guidance and care. Grandmothers who had never held a hammer in their lives could be seen industriously pounding nails. Work proceeded in the evenings when husbands leaving jobs would join their wives and children at the construction sites. It became a true community effort.

It should be pointed out that we were not creating make-work for these families. Their efforts were an essential contribution and fully complemented IBEC's in the completion of the project.

Aims Fulfilled

The houses eventually completed with the help of the Cherokee families have approximately 1,000 square feet of indoor floor space and have three or four bedrooms. Each house has covered front and back porches, a living-dining area, a complete kitchen, full bath, and utility room. Each dwelling is equipped with furnace, hot water heater, refrigerator, and range. In addition, the Public Health Service has installed a septic tank and water well.

The market value of such a house has been estimated by the local FHA office to be about $15,000. In contrast to this, the families cooperating with us had been living previously in shacks that averaged about two rooms in size. Less than half of these shacks had running water. Less than 10% had hot water, and less than 15% had central heating.

Since that initial project, IBEC has built a total of more than 375 units for the Cherokees, the Choctaws, and the Creeks, and we expect to be building at the rate of 500 units a year by 1972. From Oklahoma, we have moved into North Carolina, and we have had more requests from Indian tribal authorities than we can possibly handle.

The Indians, incidentally, have proved their critics wrong. The first families have been living in their homes for nearly three years, and the pride and care they exercise in the maintenance of their property is clearly evident. For the Indians, the project has made adequate shelter a reality at last. For our part, we have had the satisfaction of helping, in a small measure, to meet a critical problem. We played our role in a businesslike fashion and have enjoyed a fair return on our investment from the start.

The Indian housing project has been successful because IBEC scrupulously observed each of the guidelines earlier described. It identified a need clearly, developed new ways to meet it, worked out the financial requirements in detail, and adapted the venture to the social and cultural norms of the Indian families. All this is now a matter of record. Nevertheless, it is an interesting fact that IBEC has attracted few competitors. This is all the more remarkable considering the enormous market that exists for the product. We have been given estimates that, throughout the United States, there is an immediate demand for about 90,000 homes for Indians to be constructed under Mutual Self-Help Housing Programs. Apparently, this is not only a good business but a very big business as well.

Several companies have expressed an interest in our project. Unfortunately, however, the strangeness of the problems seems to discourage some from going further. For instance:

- In the IBEC developments, the houses are not set side by side, each on its own lot, as in a suburban development; IBEC's first 30 homes are separated by 157 miles, and, at first, some of the sites even lacked access roads.

- Unskilled Indian labor creates uncertainties in figuring labor costs of construction.

- The contractor must work with diverse federal agencies and community organizations.

Obviously, such requirements cannot be met by applying business formulas developed for conventional operations. Management must be businesslike—but it must also be imaginative and willing to take risks. In short, the need is for entrepreneurial vision.

The Fundamental Facts

In my judgment, we American businessmen have allowed ourselves to become too absorbed in the problem of learning how to manage and control the awesome technology that has been created by our national genius. We have turned our backs on the larger environment, both physical and societal.

The last quarter of a century has seen an unbelievable leap forward in technological achievement. The development of commercial computers, synthetic materials, color television, space flight, and other technologies has resulted in the creation of entirely new, very complex industries and new frames of reference in an extraordinarily short time span. The successful management of these new industries has imposed severe demands on executives. In response, we have developed highly sophisticated techniques of control and management, which consume much of our time and energy. To our credit, we have, by and large, succeeded admirably with that part of the job.

In doing so, however, we have neglected some fundamental facts of life. For instance, along with most other Americans, we thought that the environment no longer mattered so much, that it was controllable. But now we have learned we can no longer afford such arrogance. In addition, we are experiencing, as managers of other institutions are, mounting criticism of our policies. Are these voices—the black militants, Naderites, student revolutionaries, conservationists, pollution controllers, and other seemingly "anti-business" forces—to be considered as enemies or as signals of environmental change that indicate the emergence of a new value system and the rise of new opportunities?

Hopefully, we will regard the changing moods and interests of the public as opportunities. After all, business executives themselves have had an important hand in stimulating these new attitudes. The affluence we created, our advertising, our industrial relations philosophies, and our own insistence on the values of change— these have surely played no little part in generating the public desires of the 1970s.

Fundamental to the private enterprise system is the quality of entrepreneurship—that peculiar ability to anticipate needs and turn them into markets, to find a challenge in the discipline of balancing risks against rewards, and to look beyond the year-end figures to the greater environment in which the corporation lives. In today's world, time is running out for those who choose to conduct business by past formulas. U.S. business *can* respond creatively, *can* bring its impressive array of scientific and management technology to bear on the problems of our time. In so doing, business will retain the leadership and the respect it has earned in the past.

Originally published in January–February 1971
Reprint R0308J

The Authority of Ideas

LAWRENCE H. SUMMERS

T ODAY'S BUSINESS ORGANIZATIONS will succeed
or fail on the quality of their ideas and on the speed with
which the best of those ideas can be implemented. As
companies explore ways to do more with their ideas
and deploy their knowledge, they could do worse than
look in what might seem an unlikely place: the research
university.

What is special about the research university? Part of
the answer is that at the university, our most important
assets are not our buildings but the people of our community and the knowledge they have. Universities are
places where very talented people can come—sometimes
for short, intense periods—to work with and learn from
other very talented people. Another part of the answer is
that research universities are decentralized organizations—that is, they give their people general guidelines,
provide them with resources, and create environments in
which they can do their best work.

In this increasingly fast-paced world of information dissemination and global exchange, the idea of decentralization has consistently proven its merit. Economists argue about the way a modern national economy functions, but almost all agree that the best role for government is to provide economic incentives rather than any kind of direct coordination. The communist vision has been rejected; the socialist vision of government owning and directing the means of production has been discredited. To a large extent, the idea that government can pick and choose activities and command industry is seen as outmoded at best and counterproductive at worst.

Businesses, too, have moved a long way from the hierarchical Ford Motor Company of the 1920s, which employed a large number of people to perform repetitive tasks in precise and rapid ways to achieve a consistent objective. The weakness of centralized economies and organizations—indeed the reason history has come down on the side of decentralization—is that centralization inhibits the development and flow of ideas. And ideas are the currency of the twenty-first-century economy.

But what is most special about the American research university is that it is a place where the authority of ideas, rather than the idea of authority, reigns supreme. At Harvard, we consider it an extremely important accomplishment when a 25-year-old graduate student who has been here a mere 18 months makes a discovery that disproves the pet theory of a 55-year-old professor who has been here 30 years. Indeed, the professor whose theory has been disproved might be the first to congratulate that graduate student.

The notion that one of the community's most junior members would be applauded for upending the life's work of one of its most senior would seem exceedingly strange in many organizations and countries. Yet it is fundamental to what Harvard and other American universities are about. And if you look at the organizations in the economy where the greatest value is being added, they are increasingly the organizations that share the values and character of universities. Organizations that foster an environment where creativity is rewarded, that prepare themselves to respond to challenges and execute their strategy in a nimble way, and that discourage rigid adherence to hierarchy will best be able to meet the challenges of this new century.

About the Contributors

JONATHAN BARNEY is Managing Director of Medley Emerging Markets, a Division of Medley Global Advisors. He has a background in global strategic consulting and national security/foreign policy. He graduated with honors from the U.S. Naval Academy and received an M.B.A. from Harvard Business School.

CHRISTOPHER A. BARTLETT is the Thomas D. Casserly Jr. Professor of Business Administration at Harvard Business School. He is the author of seven books, including *Managing Across Borders: The Transnational Solution,* which was named one of the 50 most influential business books of the century by the *Financial Times*, and *The Individualized Corporation*, which was named one of the Best Business Books for the Millennium by *Strategy + Business* magazine.

NICOLAS CHECA is managing Director of Kissinger McLarty Associates in New York.

DEBRA DUNN is the Senior Vice President for Corporate Affairs at Hewlett-Packard, with leadership responsibility for HP's global-citizenship efforts. Over the past 20 years she has held a number of line and staff positions at HP including Vice President of Corporate Strategy and Operations, Division General Manager, Division Marketing Manager, and Division

Manufacturing Manager. She has an M.B.A. from Harvard Business School and a B.A. from Brown University.

SUMANTRA GHOSHAL is a Fellow of the Advanced Institute of Management (AIM) in the U.K. and a Professor of Strategy and International Management at the London Business School.

STEPHEN GREEN joined The Hongkong and Shanghai Banking Corporation Limited in 1982. In 1998, he was appointed to the position of Executive Director, Investment Banking and Markets, and in 2003, he was appointed Group Chief Executive Officer. He was educated at Oxford University and received a master's degree from Massachusetts Institute of Technology.

FRED HASSAN is Chief Executive Officer of Schering-Plough and the Director and Chairman of Schering-Plough's Board of Directors. In addition, he is chairman of the HealthCare Institute of New Jersey and serves on the Boards of Directors of Avon Products, Inc., and EDS Corporation. He received a B.S. degree in chemical engineering from the Imperial College of Science and Technology at the University of London and an M.B.A. from Harvard Business School.

ROBERT D. HORMATS is Vice Chairman of Goldman Sachs (International) and a Managing Director of Goldman, Sachs & Co. He received his A.B. from Tufts University in 1965 with a concentration in economics and political science. In 1966 he received an M.A., and in 1969, a Ph.D. in international economics from the Fletcher School of International Law and Diplomacy.

JEFFREY IMMELT is Chairman of the Board and Chief Executive Officer of General Electric.

ROSABETH MOSS KANTER is the Ernest L. Arbuckle Professor of Business Administration at Harvard Business School, specializing in strategy, innovation, and leadership for change. She is a frequent contributor to HBR and was the editor from 1989 to 1992.

KENNETH LIEBERTHAL is the William Davidson Professor of Business Administration, Professor of International Business and Corporate Strategy, and Professor of Political Science at the University of Michigan.

JOHN MAGUIRE is Head of the Emerging Markets Division of Medley Global Advisors, a political and economic consulting firm. He brings a decade of trading in global debt, currency, commodity, and derivatives markets to the firm. An avid skier, dramaturg, and fine wine collector, he lives in New Jersey with his wife.

MICHAEL MARKS is the CEO of Flextronics, a $14 billion Electronics Manufacturing Services provider, with factories in 26 countries, serving leading OEMs like Hewlett-Packard, Motorola, Siemens, Microsoft, Xerox, and others. He has two children, and enjoys playing the piano, hiking, biking, and skiing at his vacation home in Sun Valley. He is also a basketball fanatic.

DANIEL MEILAND is Executive Chairman of Egon Zehnder International, a leading global executive search firm with 58 offices worldwide. The firm is active in executive search, board appointments, and management appraisal. He holds an M.B.A. from Harvard Business School and lives in New York City.

C. K. PRAHALAD is the Harvey C. Fruehauf Professor of Business Administration at the University of Michigan Business School in Ann Arbor.

RODMAN C. ROCKEFELLER was the President and later the Chief Executive of International Basic Economy. He was also Chairman of IBEC, a successor company. He was Director of the Rockefeller Center, the New School for Social Research, and other organizations. He died in 2000.

LAWRENCE H. SUMMERS is the President of Harvard University. He is the former Nathaniel Ropes Professor of Political Economy at Harvard and a former Secretary of the U.S. Treasury.

KEITH YAMASHITA is a Cofounder and Principal of San Francisco–based Stone Yamashita Partners, which consults to companies undergoing large-scale strategic change. He worked closely with Debra Dunn to design the fused strategy described in this article.

Index

ABB. *See* Asea Brown Boveri (ABB)

Afghanistan, 58, 59

Ahold (Swiss conglomerate), 130

Albania, 50

Alfa Bank, 64

American Airlines, 104

American economy, nineteenth-century growth of. *See also* Lincoln, Abraham
  antebellum context and, 25–28
  economic opportunity and, 31–35
  economic policies and, 30–31, 33–35, 40–42
  national infrastructure and, 35–37
  relevance to globalization and, 28–31, 44–46
  role of government and, 37–40, 42–44

American Society of Clinical Oncology, 79

Arbor Acres Farm, 177–178

architect, business manager as, 94, 97–99

Argentina, 55, 60–63

Arthur Martin (French company), 95

Asea Brown Boveri (ABB), 101, 163

AT&T, 121

Avon, 79

Bajaj (Indian company), 153

Balmer, Hans, 129, 137

Bamerindus (Brazil), 73

Becton Dickinson, 104–105

BMW, 123–124, 135, 137

Boeing, 163

Boston, MA, 118, 120

BP. *See* British Petroleum (BP)

brand management, in emerging markets, 146–147, 148–149

Brazil, 46, 51
  emerging markets in, 143, 146, 147, 152, 164
  financial mobilization project in, 178–179

197